Numinous

Marguerite Horner Numinous

Foreword

It's ten years since Marguerite Horner presented her first solo exhibition at the Crypt in St Marylebone Parish Church, London. In a review of that show, *Through Each Today,* for the *Guardian,* Skye Sherwin described how in Horner's work 'everyday sights are transformed into charged, luminous moments'.[1] While the western coastline of the USA presented in this new exhibition is perhaps not an everyday sight for Horner's fellow Londoners, the same sense of 'charged, luminous moments' defines the artist's latest series of paintings, *Numinous.*

The title offers a clue as to what that mysterious charge might be – the presence of the otherworldly or the spiritual. In this series of twenty-one watercolours, accompanied by two oil paintings, the viewer encounters cloudless skies, distant horizons, gently undulating waves lapping at the shore, untouched sand and picturesque rocks, and verdant – occasionally cactus-filled – foliage anchoring the compositions in the foreground. It is difficult to imagine a place closer to paradise, and in such sublime locations our minds can wander from quotidian, earthly matters to thoughts of the heavenly, the eternal and the divine.

Yet the works remain grounded in the worldly, whether through signs of civilisation, such as hilltop fencing and beach huts, or the human figures peppered throughout, reduced to tiny silhouettes against the breathtaking backdrop of the natural world. Physical matter, shaped by powerful geological and elemental forces over millions of years, puts the fleeting dominance of humans and the Anthropocene into perspective, the monochromatic pigment and impressive chiaroscuro of Horner's watercolours and oil paintings adding to this sense of humanity in sharp relief from the landscape. The sunlight, air, water and earth depicted are the basic conditions for human life, and it's hard not to conceive of this body of work as a reminder that we are custodians of this planet, blessed with all we need to survive and to thrive. The presence of a coastal road, bustling with cars and SUVs in one painting, poses questions about our post-industrial world and the effects we are having on the planet.

It is my pleasure to introduce readers to Horner's publication and exhibition, and to such a poetic, meditative body of work. We are grateful to Matthew Holman for his illuminating essay and to the Revd Canon Dr Stephen Evans, Rector of St Marylebone, for hosting the exhibition. Having spent many years serving in the Royal Navy before reading theology and training for ministry, these coastal seascapes will undoubtedly have a special resonance for him. Horner and Holman both reference the German Lutheran theologian Rudolf Otto, who in one of his letters written whilst travelling in North Africa in 1911, wrote: 'Down below the broad, roaring waves of the sea break against the deep foundation of the rock. But high above the mountain, the sea, and the peaks of rock the eternal ornamentation blooms silently from the dark depths of the universe'.[2] Beyond Horner's sunny skies, the rest of the universe awaits.

Matt Price
Publisher at Hurtwood

1 Skye Sherwin, 'Chloë Brown, Peter Doig, Sean Edwards: the week's art shows in pictures', *Guardian*, 2 Aug. 2013. https://www.theguardian.com/artanddesign/gallery/2013/aug/02/exhibitionist-art-shows-3-aug (accessed 18 Sept. 2023)

2 Rudolf Otto, *Autobiographical and Social Essays*, ed. and trans. Gregory D. Alles, Berlin and New York: Mouton de Gruyter, 1996, p.73.

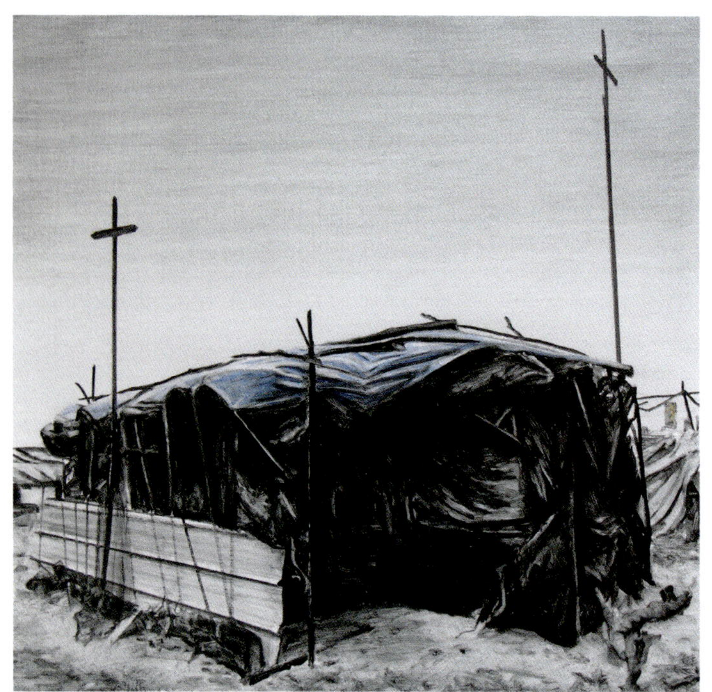 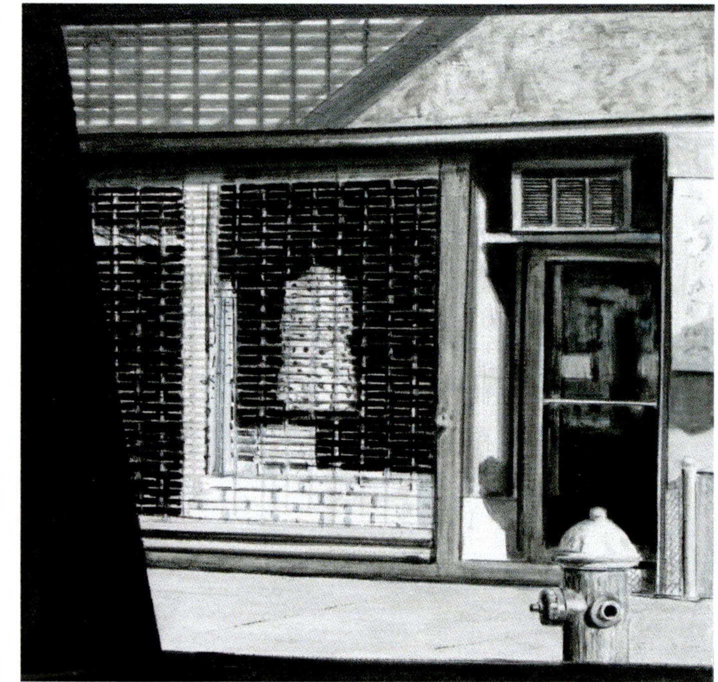

1 Marguerite Horner, *Church*, 2017, from the *Keep Me Safe* series, oil on linen, 50 x 50 cm (19 11/16 x 19 11/16 in.)
2 Marguerite Horner, *Caged*, 2013, from the *Back to Verve* series, oil on linen, 50 x 50 cm (19 11/16 x 19 11/16 in.)

Facing West   **by Matthew Holman**

Facing west from California's shores,
Inquiring, tireless, seeking what is yet unfound,
I, a child, very old, over waves, towards the house of maternity,
the land of migrations, look afar,
Look off the shores of my Western sea, the circle almost circled;
[…]
Now I face home again, very pleas'd and joyous,
(But where is what I started for so long ago?
And why is it yet unfound?)

– Walt Whitman, 'Facing West from California's Shores'[1]

Last July, I drove from Oakland to Los Angeles. If you have taken the Pacific Coast Highway (and not the Central Valley, which resembles driving through an endless gas station that has taken up a side hustle as a slaughterhouse), the heavenly westward views will be seared into your retina. From the vantage point of the snaking road, about 300 feet above sea level, the Pacific stretches out as though Yves Klein had tipped a suburban depot's worth of IKB onto an infinite white tarpaulin. What struck me most was not how blue the sky was, nor how blue the water was, but how the intermingling of sea and shoreline served as some kind of restless boundary between me – in love, on my first visit to California, in between jobs – and the vast, otherworldly colour beyond. It was as though there was a faint and mutable line between the world of activity and agency, of life as I knew it, and something radically unknowable. It was this something unknowable that seemed to threaten, in the best possible sense of the word, everything that I knew to be important and that populated my waking consciousness. That feeling is the subject of Marguerite Horner's most recent body of work, *Numinous*, a corpus dedicated to the beautified Californian coastline and how far transcendence might seem even when it's right there in front of us.

Horner's paintings are interested in lifting the seemingly banal into extraordinary states of religiosity. A devout but critical Catholic, Horner finds God in the unlikeliest of places. I first came across Horner's work in the *Keep Me Safe* series (2017), inspired by her experiences driving the Chiswick Comboni nuns and their prayer group from London to the Calais 'Jungle' refugee camp. Portraits as well as landscapes, these were pictures of hope and despair, snapshots of a world-within-a-world that is both ignored and shamelessly vilified. It was as though by offering herself into intimate engagements with strangers, Horner took the problem of ever knowing another person as the starting point for probing how well we know ourselves. More recently, the *Back to Verve* exhibition, shown at the Chelsea Arts Club in autumn 2022, established aspects of the monochrome palette, as well as sight-lines and plays in perspective, that formally structure the *Numinous* series. Largely seen from high-up, these small-town paintings find us lost in the existential dread of suburbia, or the living ruins of emaciated oak trees, or the solemn tenor of the grocery store closed at midday. They are alive and dead at the same time, signifying nothing but holding a place. Horner has always been a keen observer who depicts the most transient of places in moments when they become, against themselves, sites of possibility. In many ways, *Numinous*

1   Walt Whitman, 'Facing West from California's Shores', *Leaves of Grass*, Glasgow:
    Wilson & McCormick, 1884, p.95.

feels like the culmination of these concerns. After spending a fortnight with her daughter, an actor, one Christmastime in Beachwood Canyon, during which she took the train up and down to Del Mar, Horner produced a body of twenty-one wondrous watercolours and two oils in monochrome. The Californian coast is shown as a spectral figure that gets close to us, about as close as painting can get to a representation of another world, while remaining an uncompromising depiction of this one.

'Numinous' is the name of something very specific and yet difficult to define. It's a concept that indicates the presence of divinity. 'The feeling of it may at times come sweeping like a gentle tide pervading the mind', wrote the Lutheran theologian Rudolf Otto, who sought to define this ineffable experience through the metaphor of water: 'It may become the hushed, trembling, and speechless humility of the creature in the presence of— whom or what? In the presence of that which is a Mystery inexpressible.'[2] In other words, 'numinous' refers to a state of awe, dread or a general sense of experiencing something otherworldly. Otto's words rhyme, in many ways, with the experience of encountering a painting by Horner. That is not because the forms themselves exceed our understanding or reference – after all, they are paintings of the seashore, a familiar subject in the history of art – but because they are profoundly mysterious as a sequence. It's impossible not to see the works as in conversation with one another, as variations on a theme, but a theme that remains elusive. There's a rhythm here, like the slow caress of the wave's lip on Del Mar sands, but each work, like each wave, contains its own multitudes. The foaming build-up in *My Name Is Whisper* (2023, p.15) is different to the glassy blocks of ice-blue water in *Beyond Conceiving* (2023, p.27) despite their identical perspective, and yet each painting holds a shared mystery: why are we here? Who are these figures that walk on the sand? Why are we compelled to look so closely?

Horner's titles are often inspired by scriptural passages. *The Desert Had Turned to Sea* (2023) refers to Psalm 107:35 when God transforms the parched land into 'pools of water and [...] flowing springs.'[3] From a barren wasteland, God blessed a bounty with providence. The painting itself marks this miraculous change, a change that happens every day, as the shoreline and the Pacific kiss and part, kiss and part. (Writing this essay as Hurricane Hilary brings widespread flooding and fatal mudslides across the southwestern United States, I'm also conscious of the title as a kind of commentary on the trans- formations of southern California during a time of escalating ecological crisis.) Other paintings' titles, like *The Answer Is You* (2023, p.37), also from the *Numinous* series, resemble fragments of a lyric poem. (The title is actually taken from a line in 'Call It Something Nice', a song by Small Faces.) The titular 'You' stands as the undefined viewer (us), or perhaps a lover or even God, or even the solace that a nameless stranger might offer at a time of crisis. Perhaps, then, the young boy exercising on the beach is the addressee of this poem in paint: seen flush between two outstretched branches, which resemble his own swaying on the monkey bars, he stares toward the western horizon line. We share with him the same view, the same place, but not the same perspective; his subjectivity remains elusive to us.

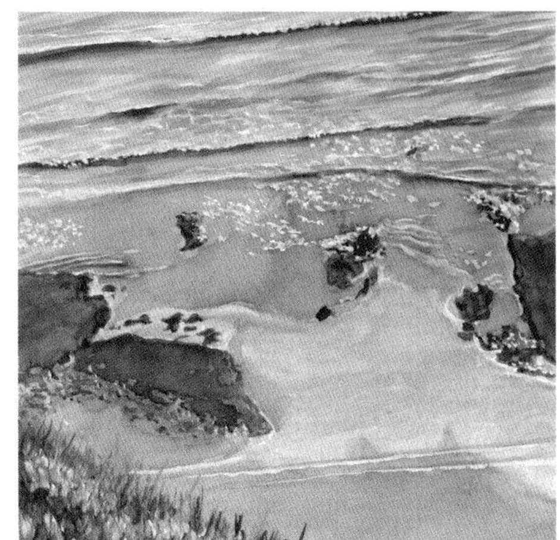

3

10

2 Rudolf Otto, *Das Heilige*, 1917, as *The Idea of the Holy: An Inquiry into the Non-Relational Factor in the Idea of the Divine and Its Relation to the Rational*, ed. John W. Harvey, New York: Oxford University Press, 1958, pp.12–13.
3 The Holy Bible: Psalms 107:35. New International Version.

Beyond the boy, the water flickers in the dappled sunlight. 'I'm thinking about tone, not colour', Horner tells me, and it is extraordinary that the two oil paintings, *I Fell into the Water* and *Refuge of the Roads* (both 2023, pp.73, 71), were produced with just two colours, Madder brown and Prussian blue, which manage to be both warm and cool simultaneously. For the watercolours, Horner used just one colour: Paynes grey, which has a blue tinge. Horner's paintings achieve much by reducing the materials of their composition: sparse colours, a single subject, multiplied. It is not by coincidence that Prussian blue was the same pigment that James McNeill Whistler used in his abstract landscapes of the Thames. Looking at *Transcends Reason and Thought* (2023), I'm reminded of Whistler's recalcitrant abstraction. Spend time with Horner's painting: notice how it's as though we see two fields of action, the blotted build-up of touches in the upper half of the sea and the overflowing ease of the lower, its spillage on the beach. Both take on abstract qualities and without the two figures taking a twilight walk, we may not see this as a painting of a coastline at all but rather a celebration of the world's forms, soft and hard, opaque and transparent. As an artist, Horner has a remarkable touch that coalesces a grain of sand and the vastness of the sea: to, in the words of Walt Whitman, witness 'the circle almost circled'.

The *Numinous* series has compositional precedents in American painting. As we discussed *Unapproachable Light* (2023, p.13), Horner mentioned the influence of Andrew Wyeth. Wyeth's deserted landscapes, I first thought, have a different atmosphere or 'tone'. His are paintings that echo across the vast, empty plains of Pennsylvania; they are melancholy and unnerving, and are fundamentally *hibernal* paintings. In short, they seem a continent and two seasons away from the leisurely blues of Horner's seascapes. And yet there is clearly a shared programme, something that binds the two painters together. Looking closer at *Unapproachable Light*, and recalling that this monochrome vista is a winter scene, even in a part of southern California that has no winters, I'm reminded of one of Wyeth's pithy statements on art-making: 'I prefer winter and fall, when you feel the bone structure in the landscape [...] Something waits beneath it; the whole story doesn't show.'[4] In Horner's painting, three figures walk at the very tip of the waves which saddle in, one after the other, as waves are wont to do, but the whole story doesn't show. The white heat of the sun blinds the overlapping waves, the figures walk, and yet from where we stand, up in the grassy foothills that loom over the beach, we know little. We feel but do not know. Horner has a remarkable ability to elicit in the viewer a profound feeling of not knowing that is not the same as ignorance. Part of this singular atmosphere is created by perspective: the figures are small because they are far from us, and they are far from us because we are looking from a distant ledge over the beach. They are absolute strangers, and yet we can see ourselves, being seen, in them. The tyranny of subject positions once more. If this series can tell us anything about the 'numinous', about the presence of the divine in places, things and people that are distant from us, and about the forms of life that exist at the very edge of the world, then they are also definitively paintings about closeness. Closeness to what or whom: well, that is a mystery we do not yet know.

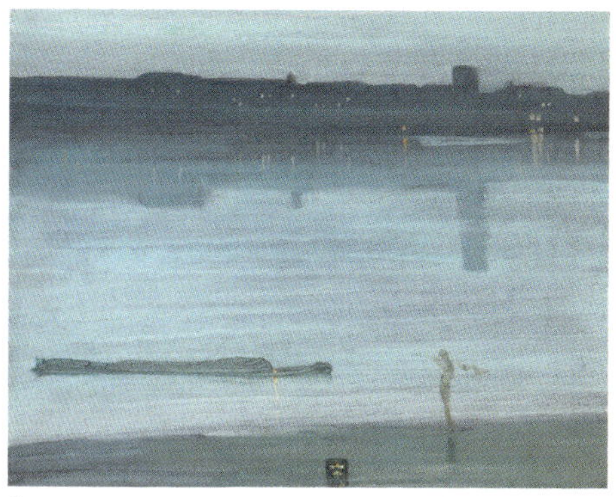

4

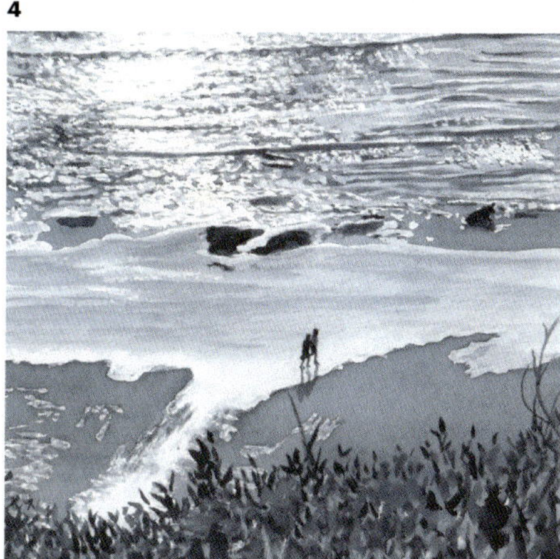

5

3 Marguerite Horner, *The Desert Had Turned to Sea*, 2023, watercolour on paper, 20 x 20 cm (7 7/8 x 7 7/8 in.)

4 James Abbott McNeill Whistler, *Nocturne: Blue and Silver – Chelsea*, 1871, oil paint on wood, 50.2 x 60.8 cm (19 3/4 x 24 in.). Tate, bequeathed by Miss Rachel and Miss Jean Alexander 1972. Photo: Tate

5 Marguerite Horner, *Transcends Reason and Thought*, 2023, watercolour on paper, 20 x 20 cm (7 7/8 x 7 7/8 in.)

4 Andrew Wyeth, cited in 'American painter Andrew Wyeth dies at 91' by Associated Press, *Guardian*, 16 Jan. 2009.
https://www.theguardian.com/artanddesign/2009/jan/16/andrew-wyeth-death-art-usa (accessed 13 Sept. 2023)

Unapproachable Light, 2023
Watercolour on paper, 20 x 20 cm (7 ⅞ x 7 ⅞ in.)

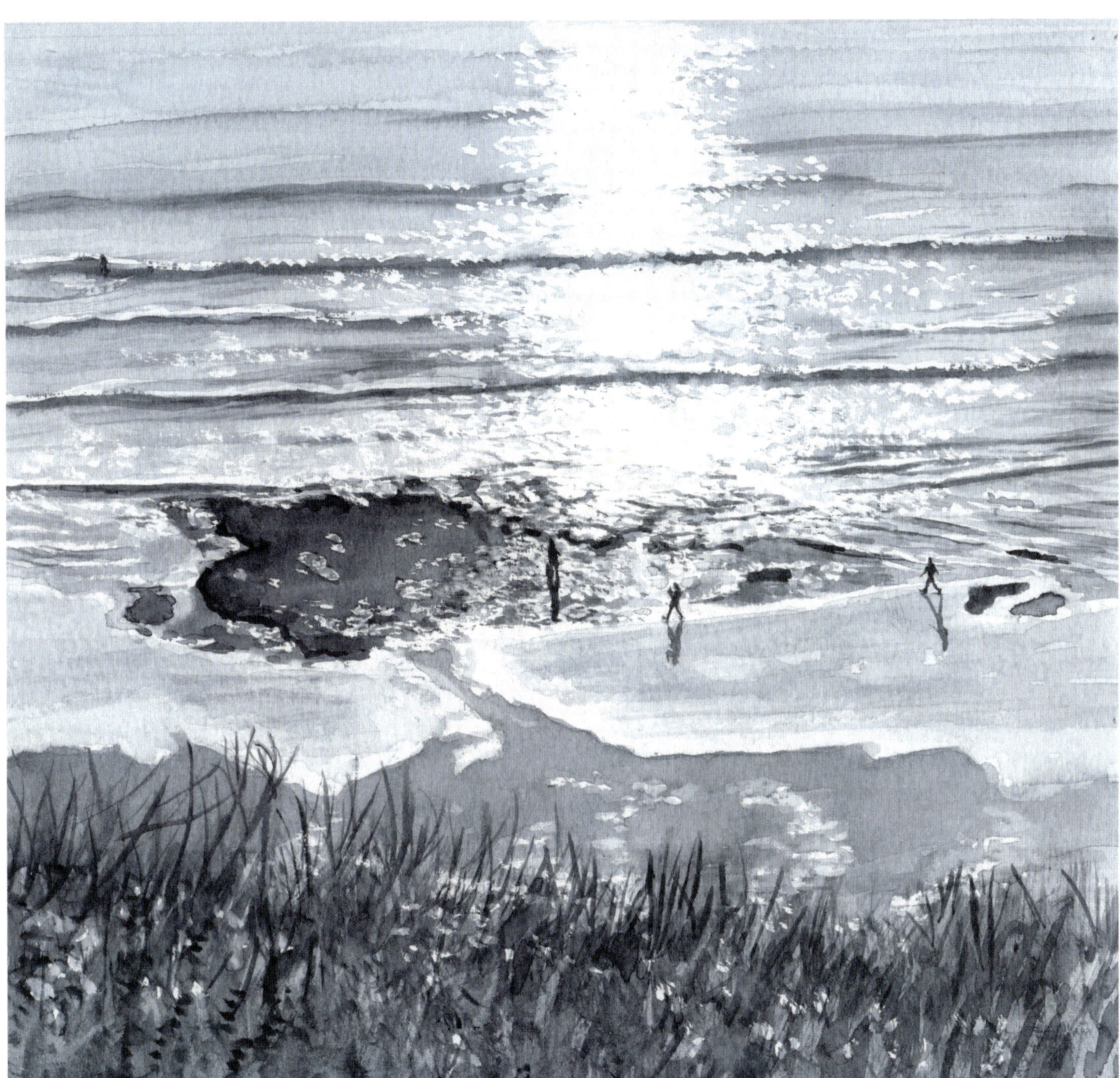

My Name Is Whisper, 2023
Watercolour on paper, 20 x 20 cm (7 ⅞ x 7 ⅞ in.)

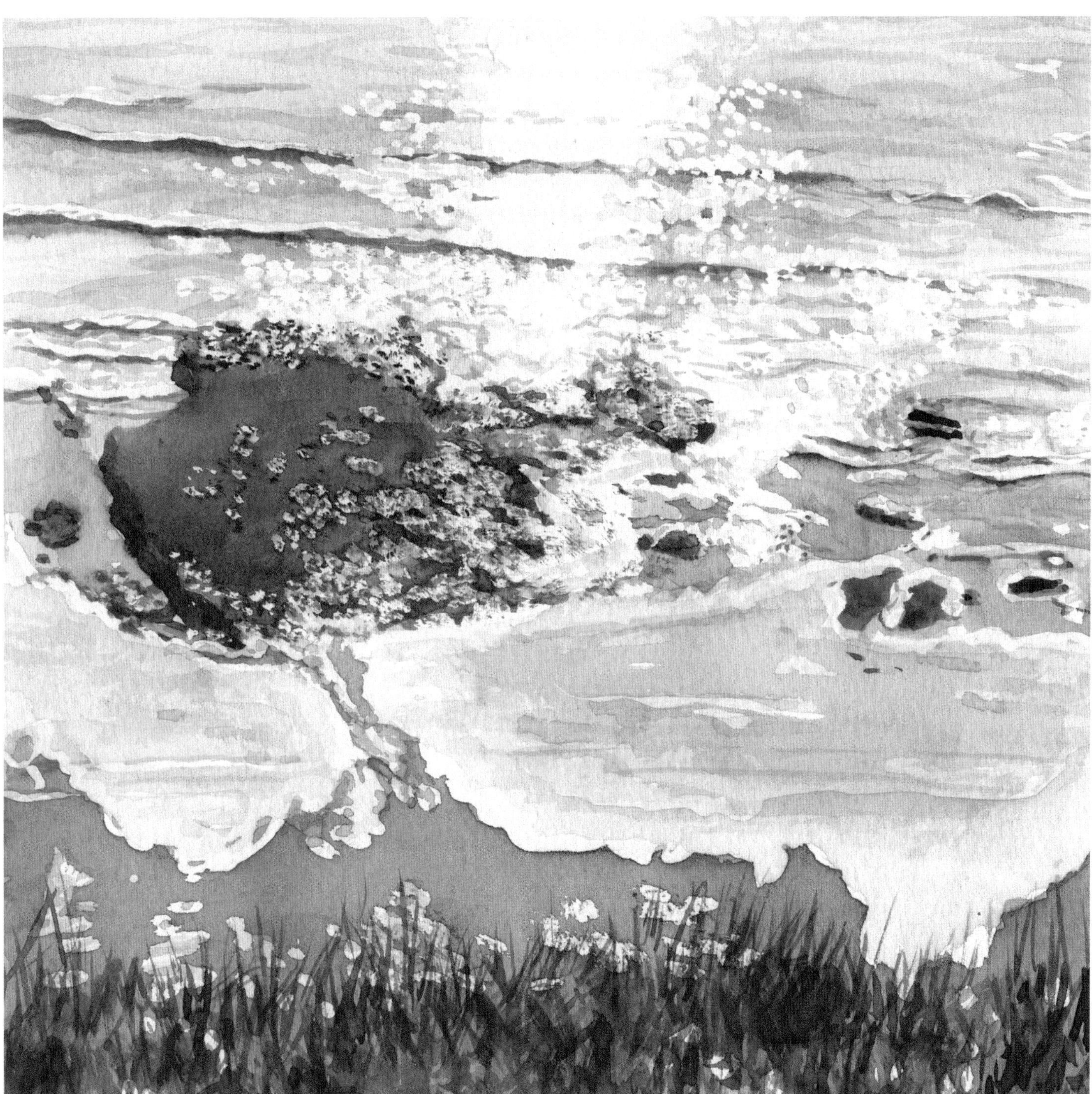

Think with Your Heart, 2023
Watercolour on paper, 20 x 20 cm (7 ⅞ x 7 ⅞ in.)

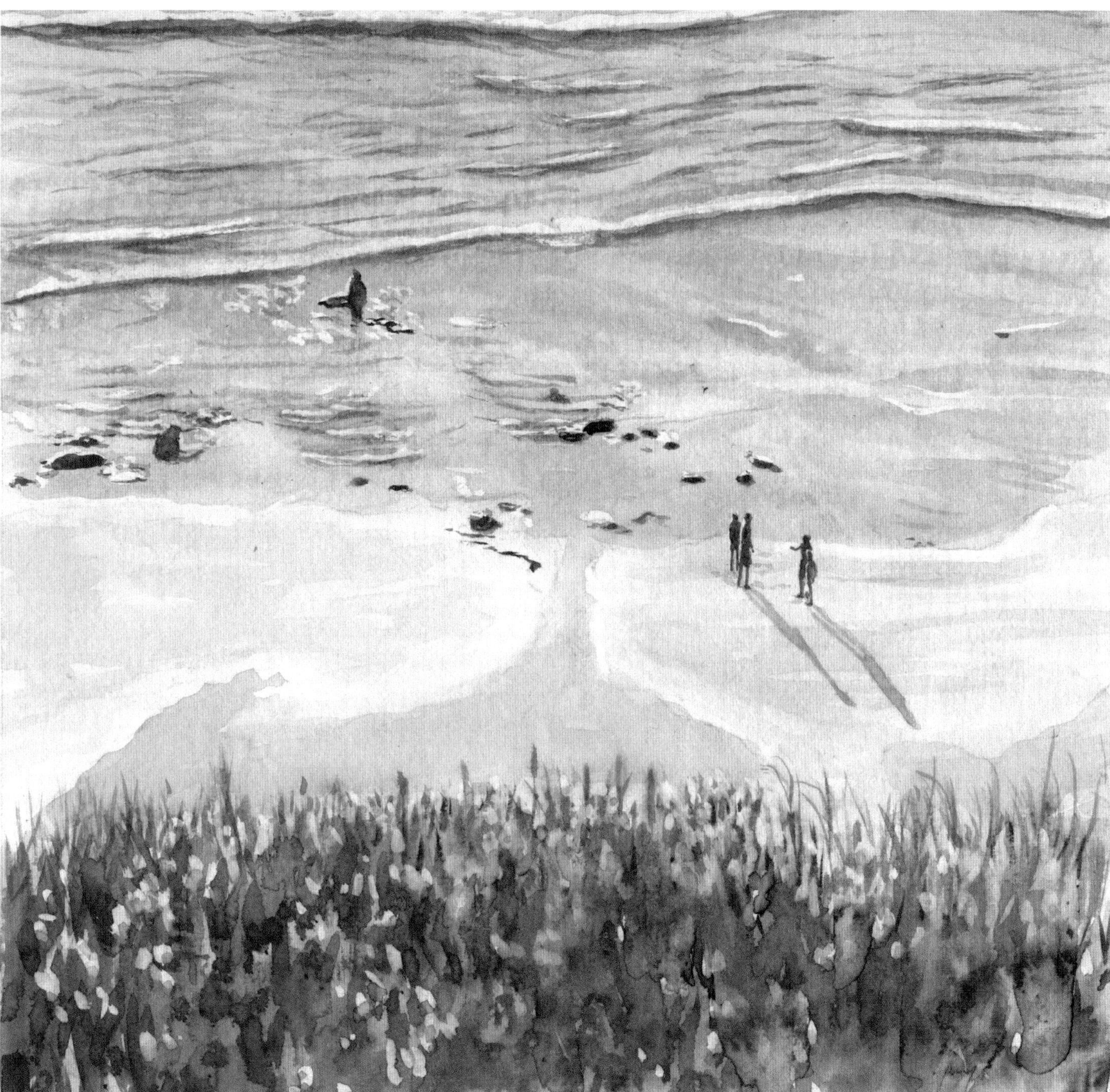

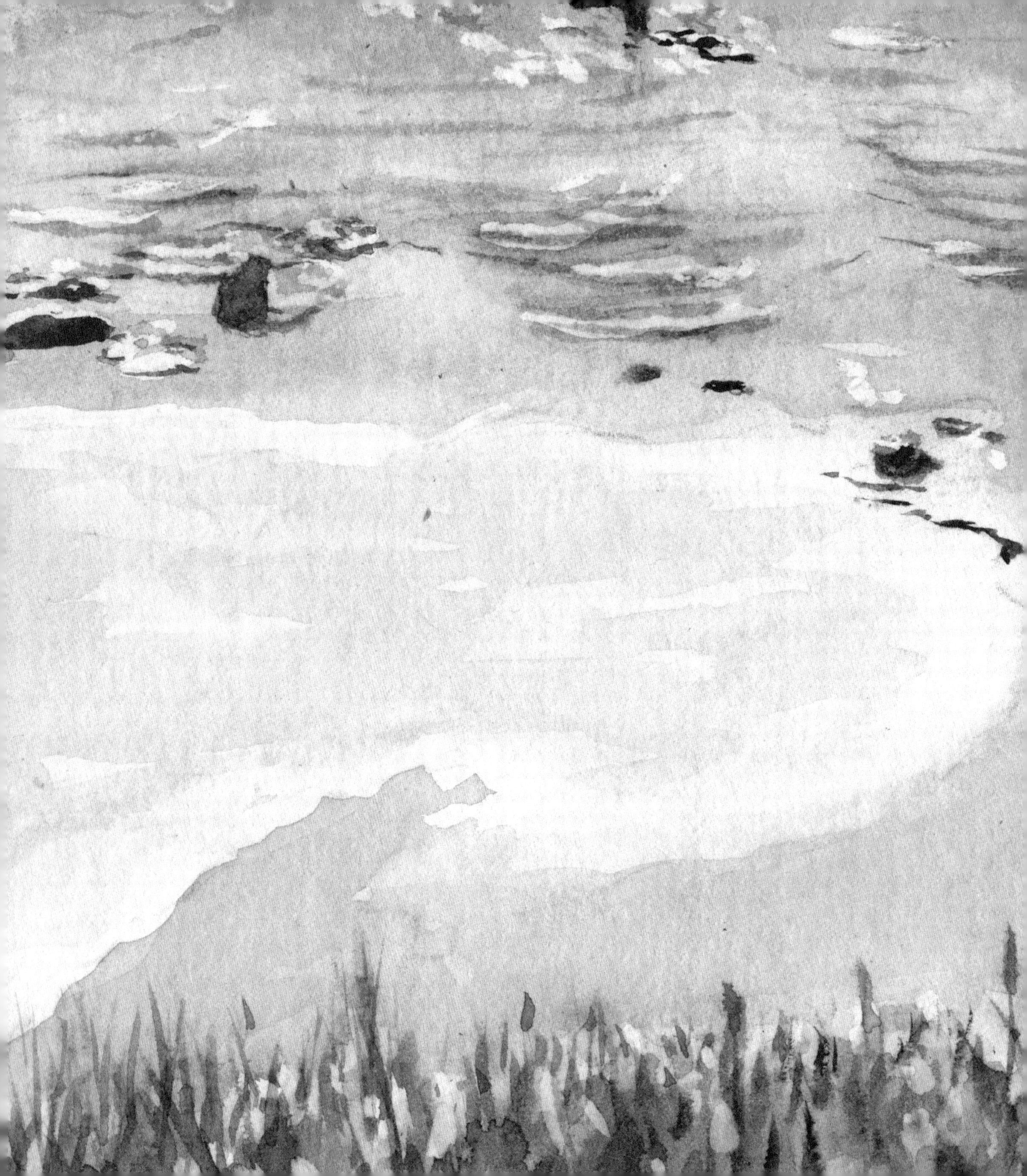

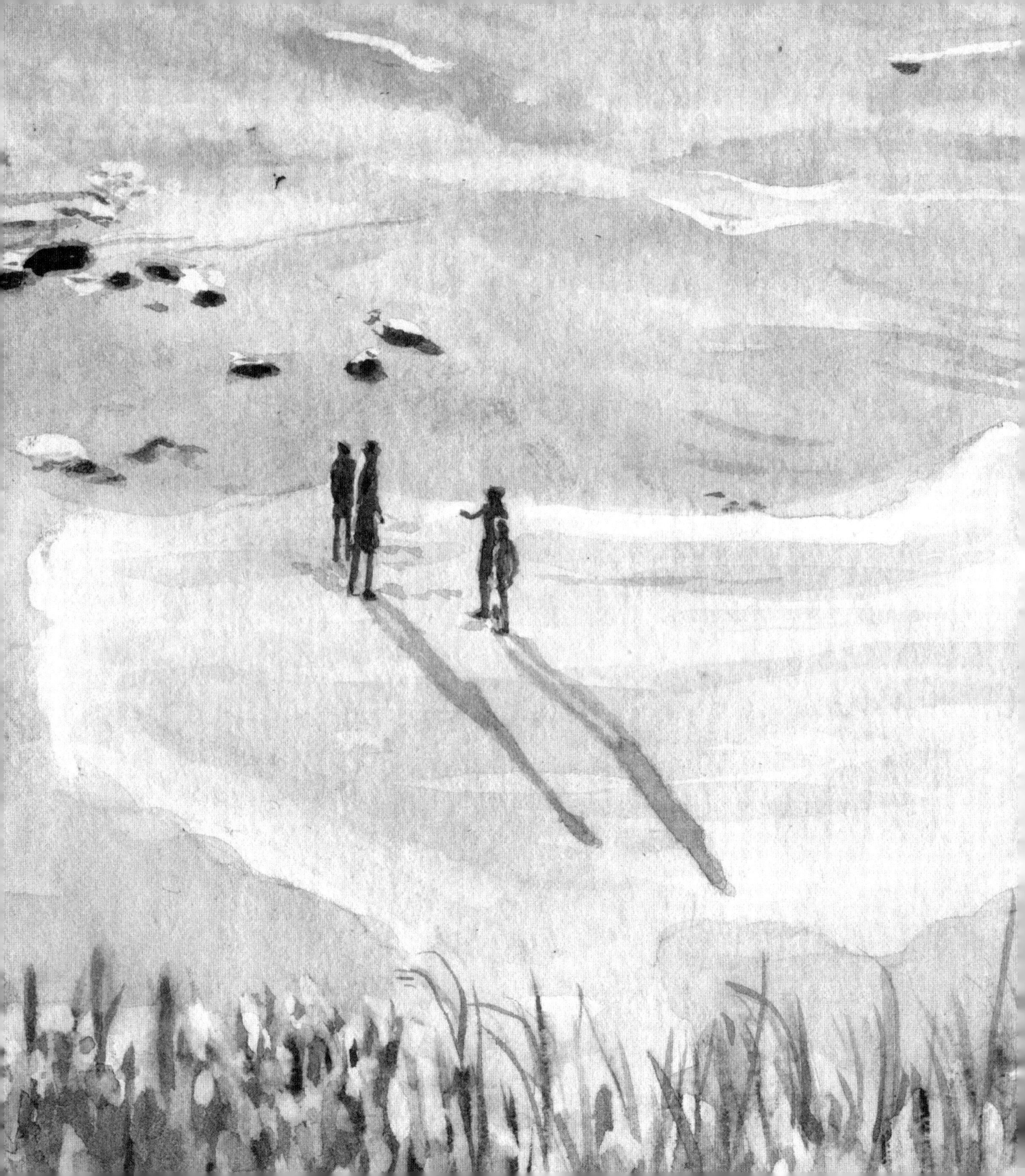

A Light Thrill, 2023
Watercolour on paper, 20 x 20 cm (7 ⅞ x 7 ⅞ in.)

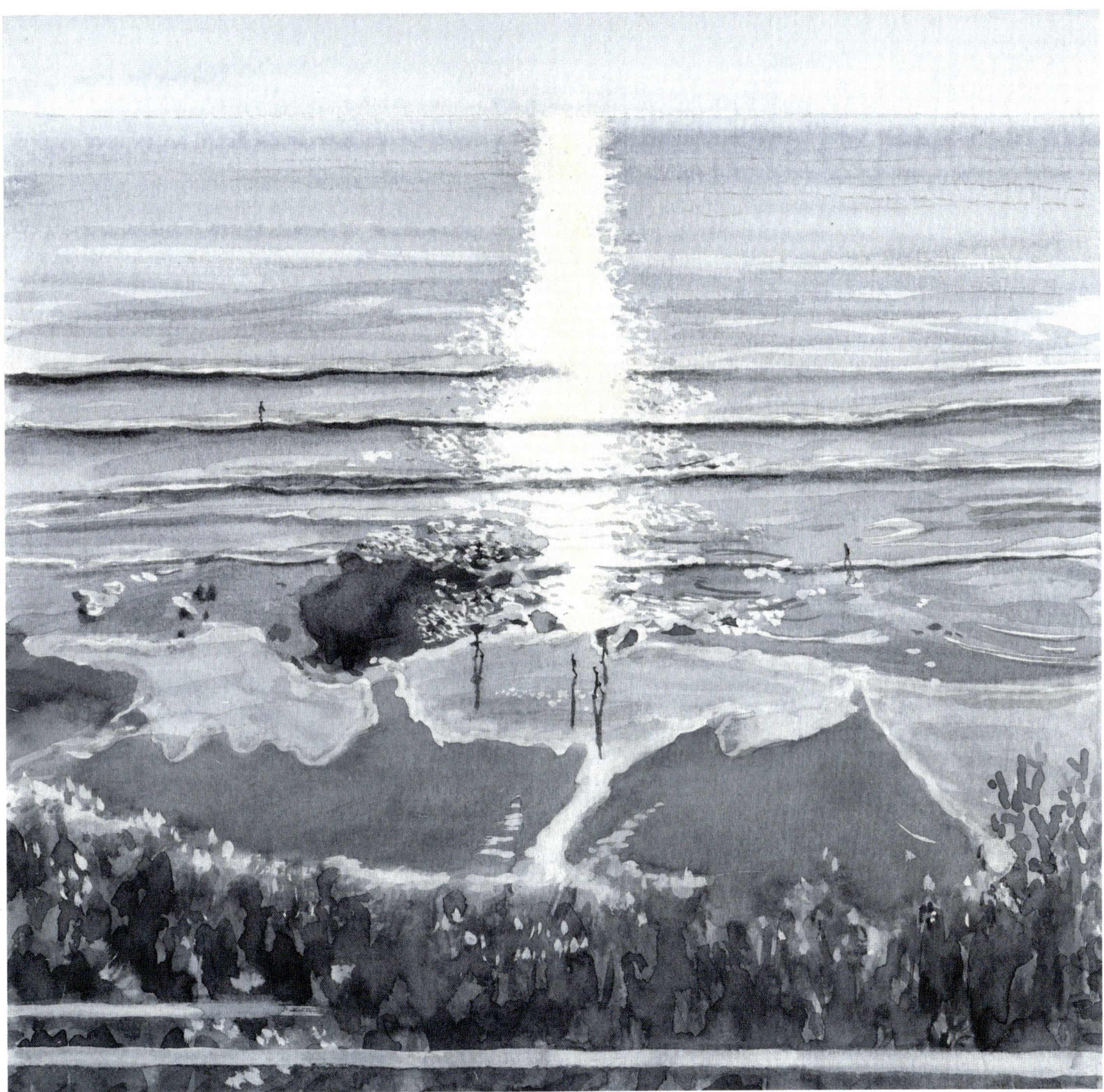

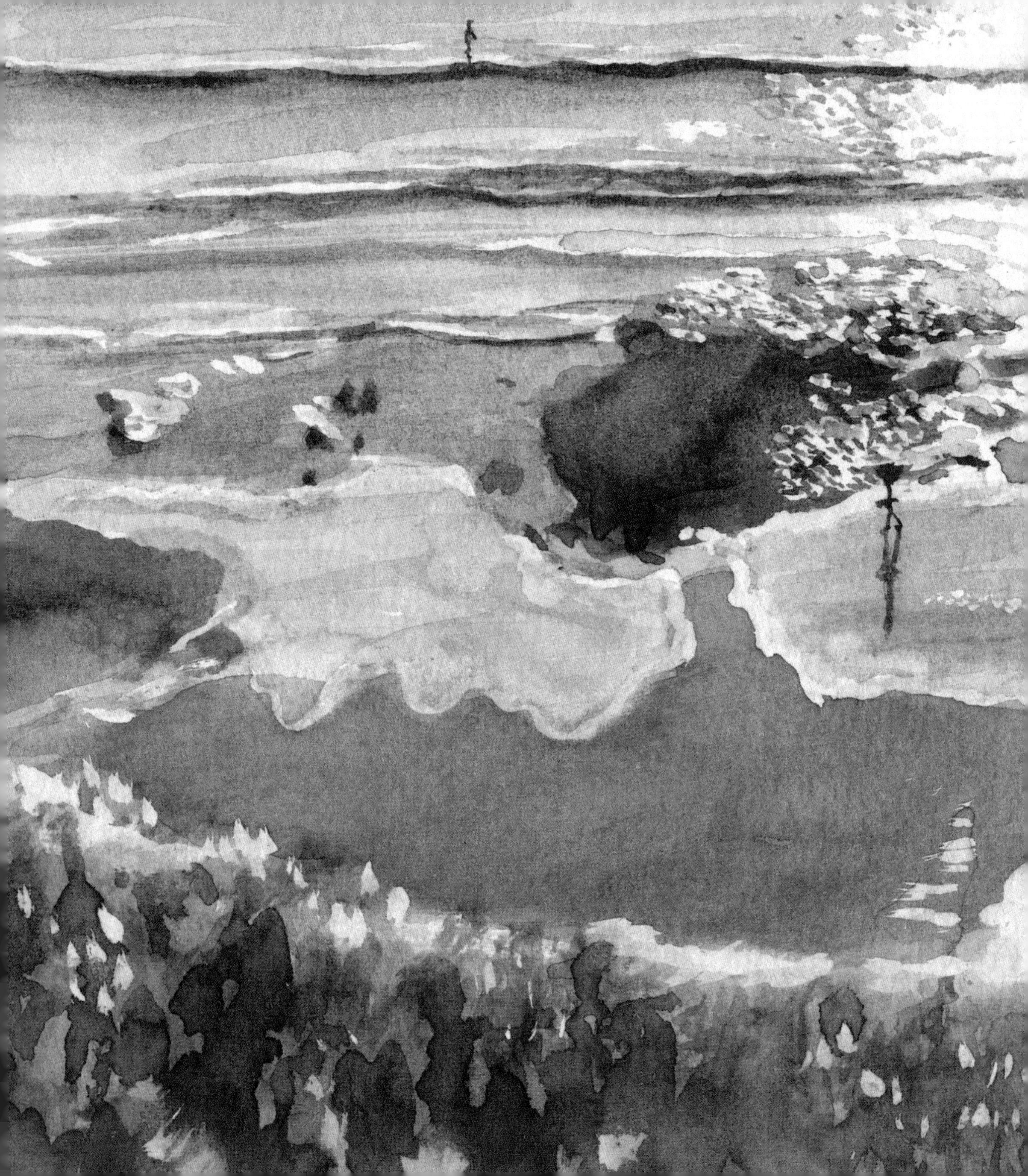

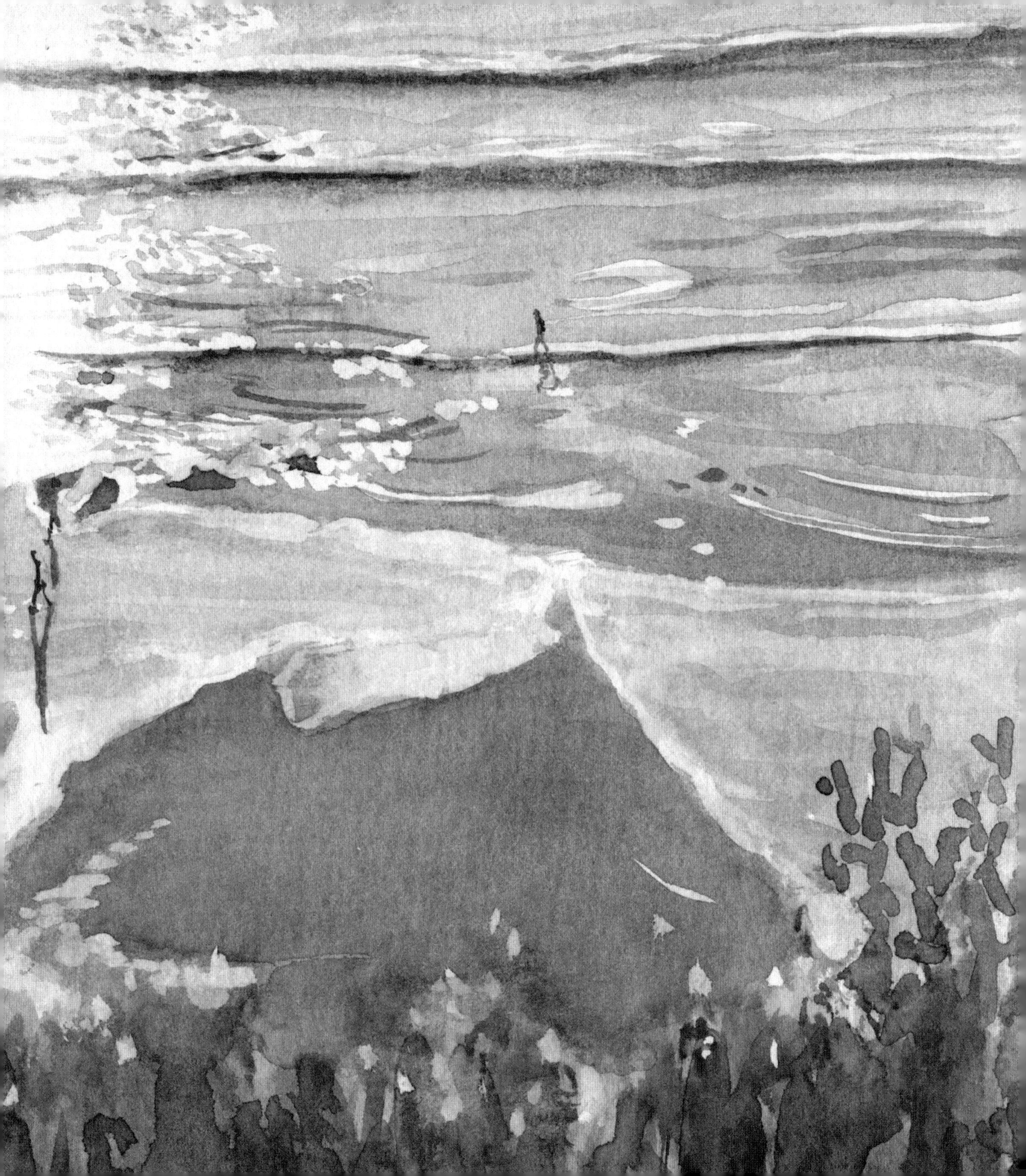

Priori Category of Mind, 2023
Watercolour on paper, 20 x 20 cm (7 ⅞ x 7 ⅞ in.)

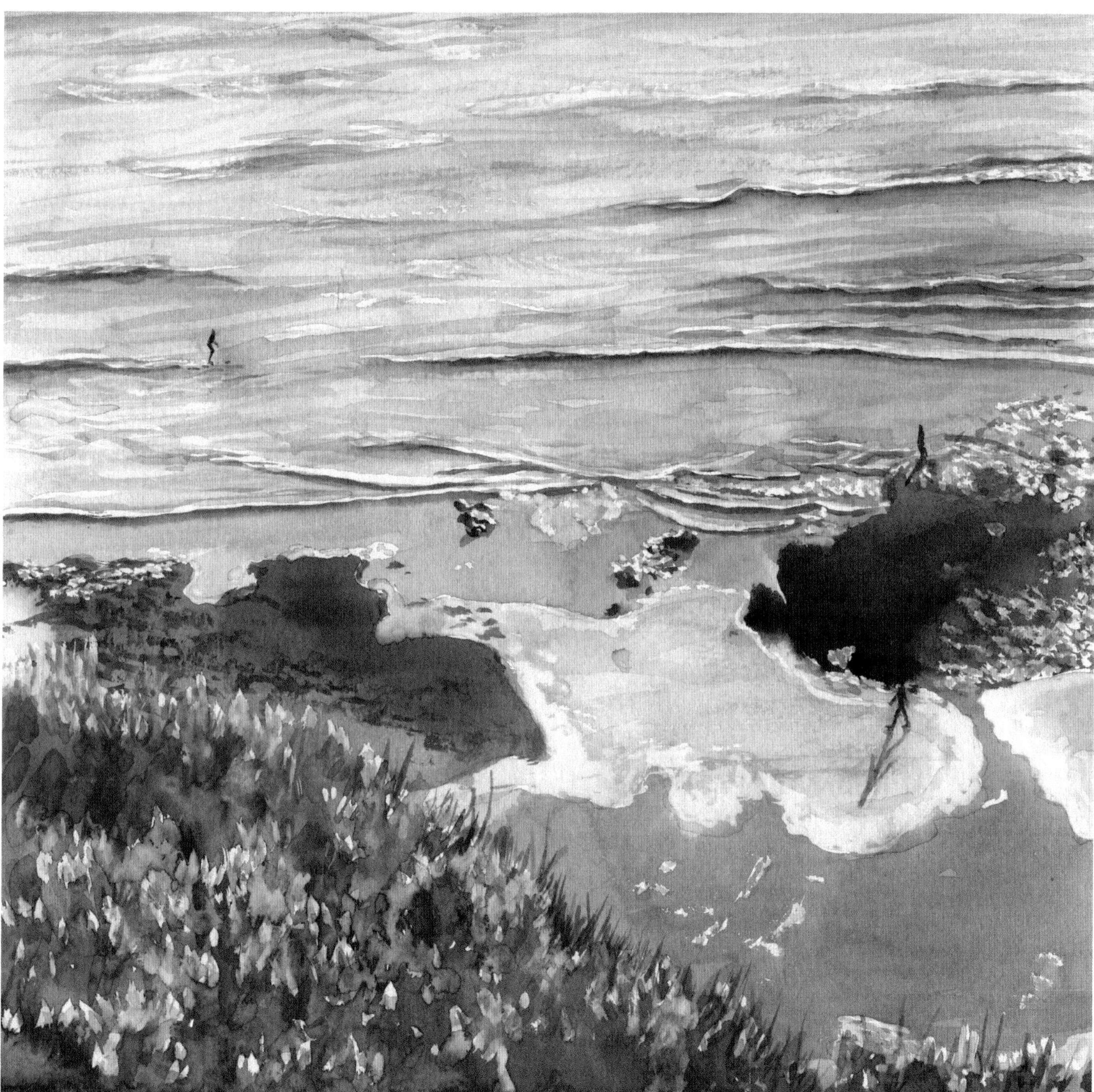

Beyond Conceiving, 2023
Watercolour on paper, 20 x 20 cm (7 ⅞ x 7 ⅞ in.)

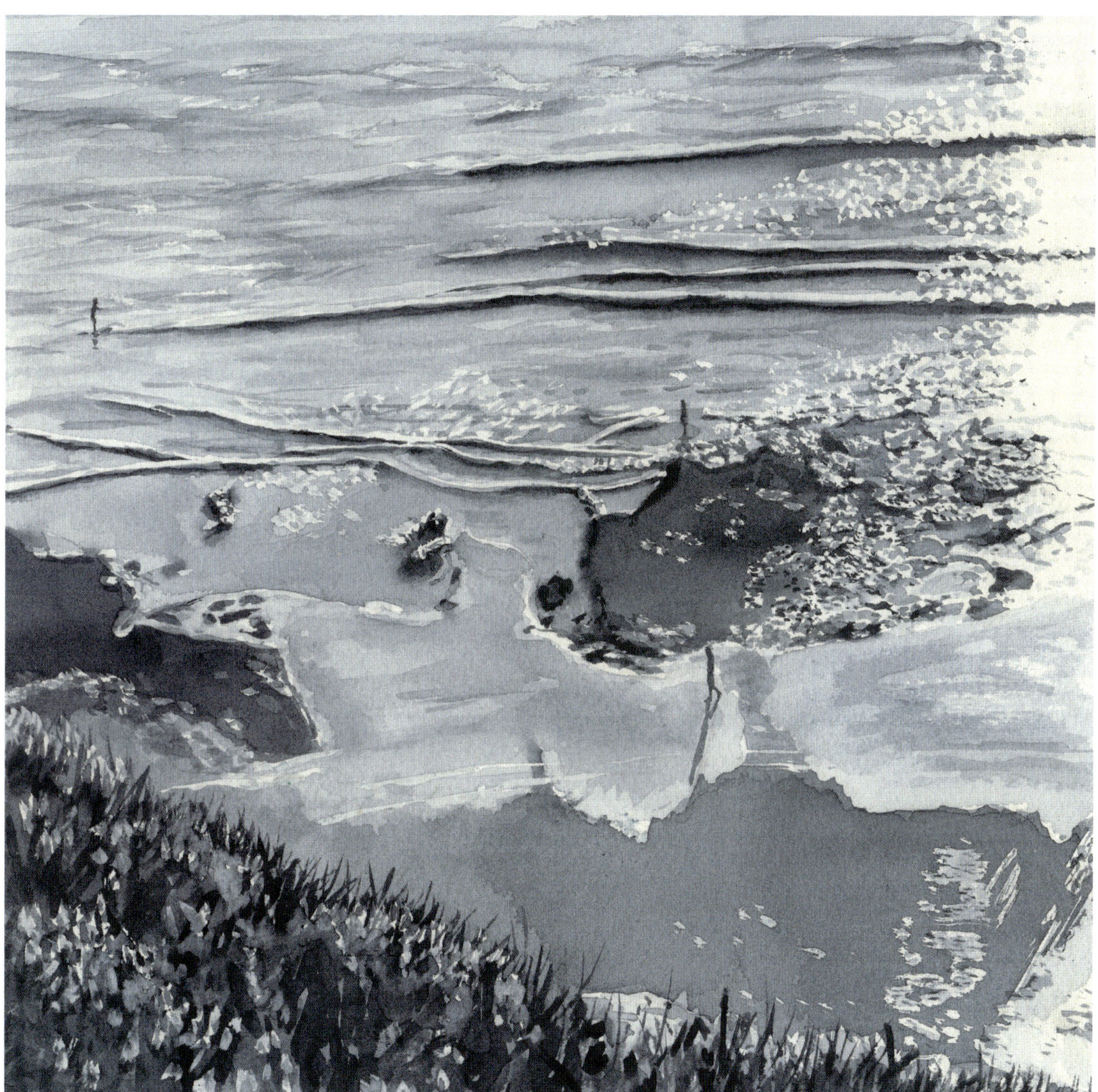

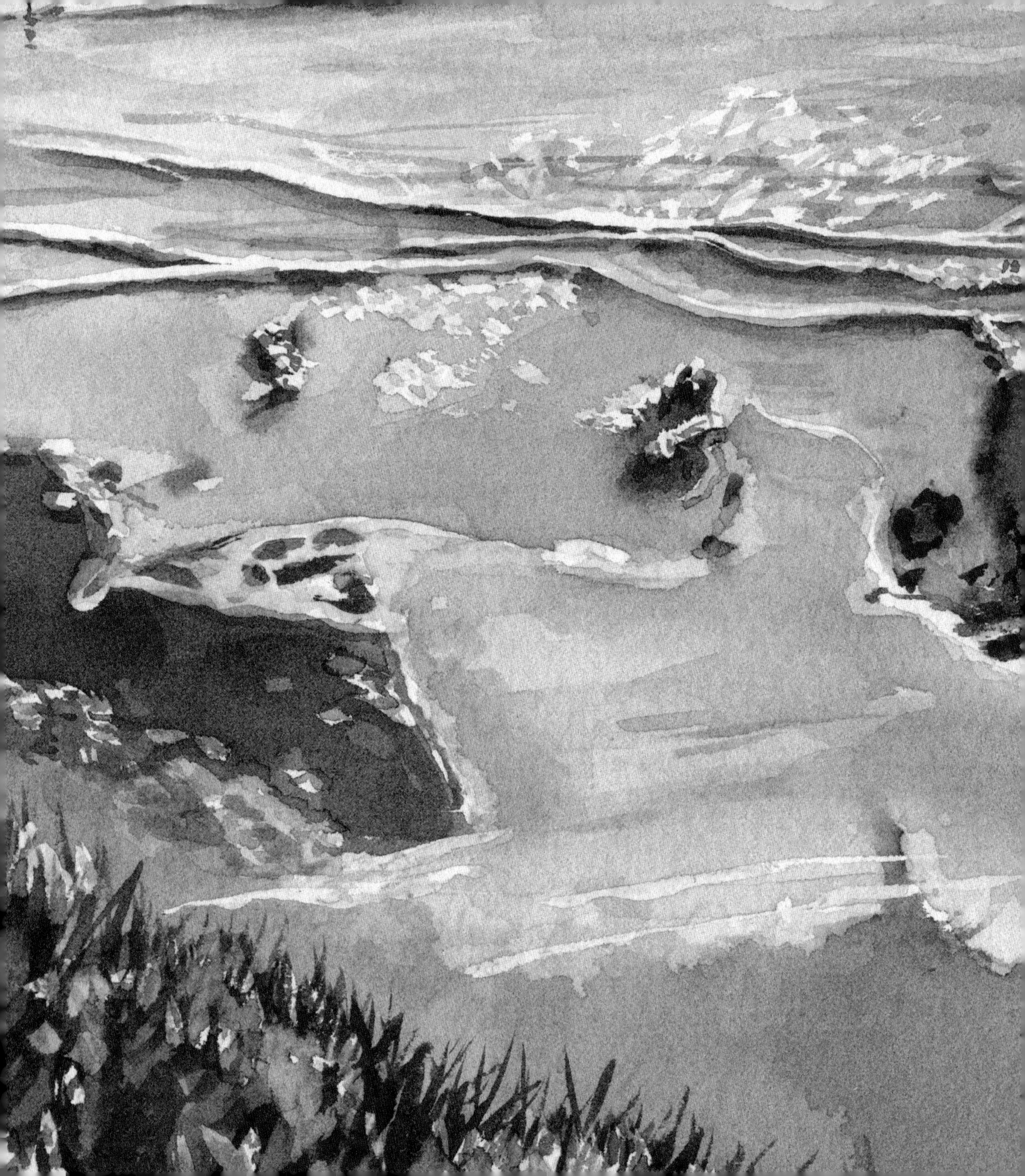

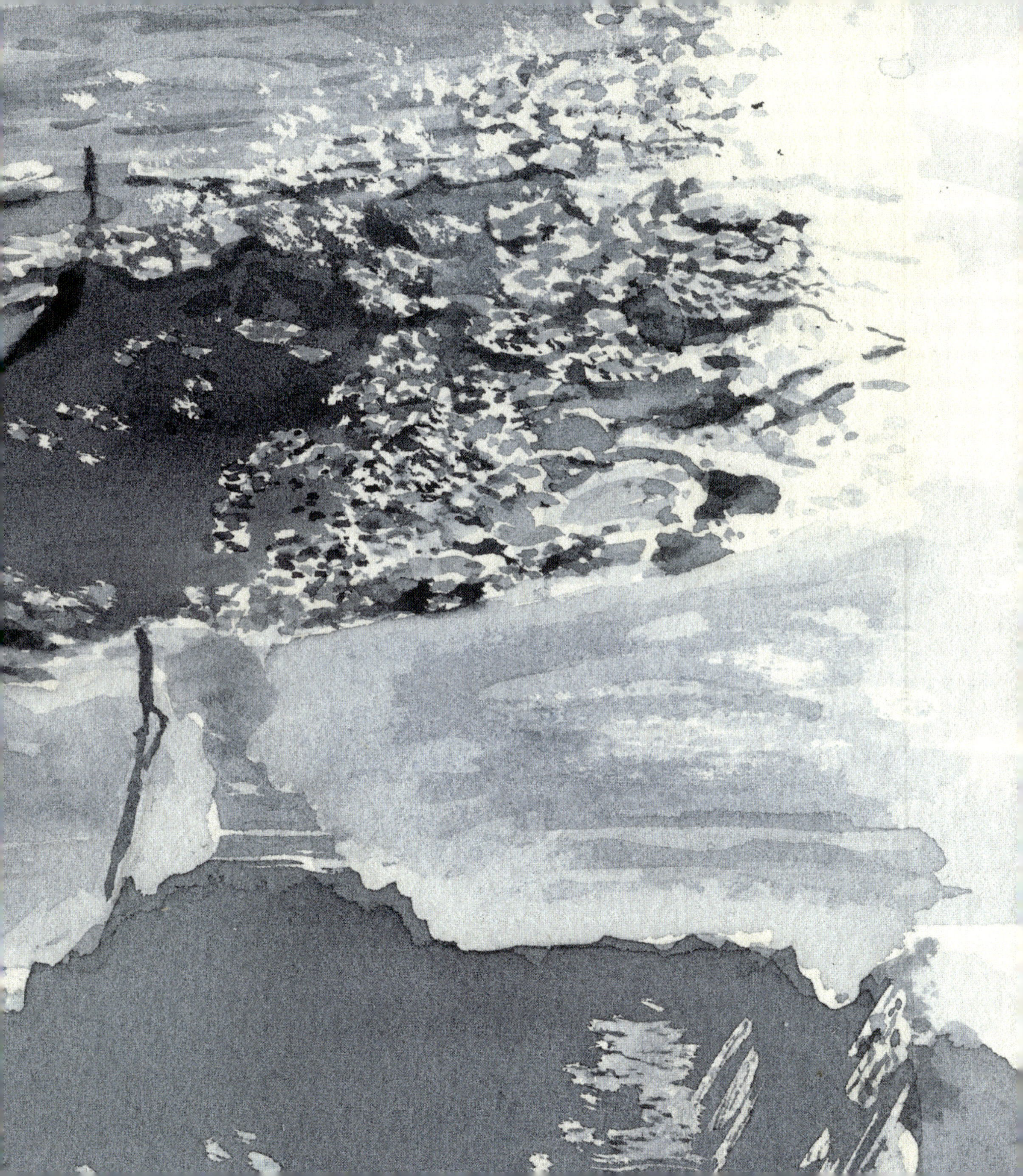

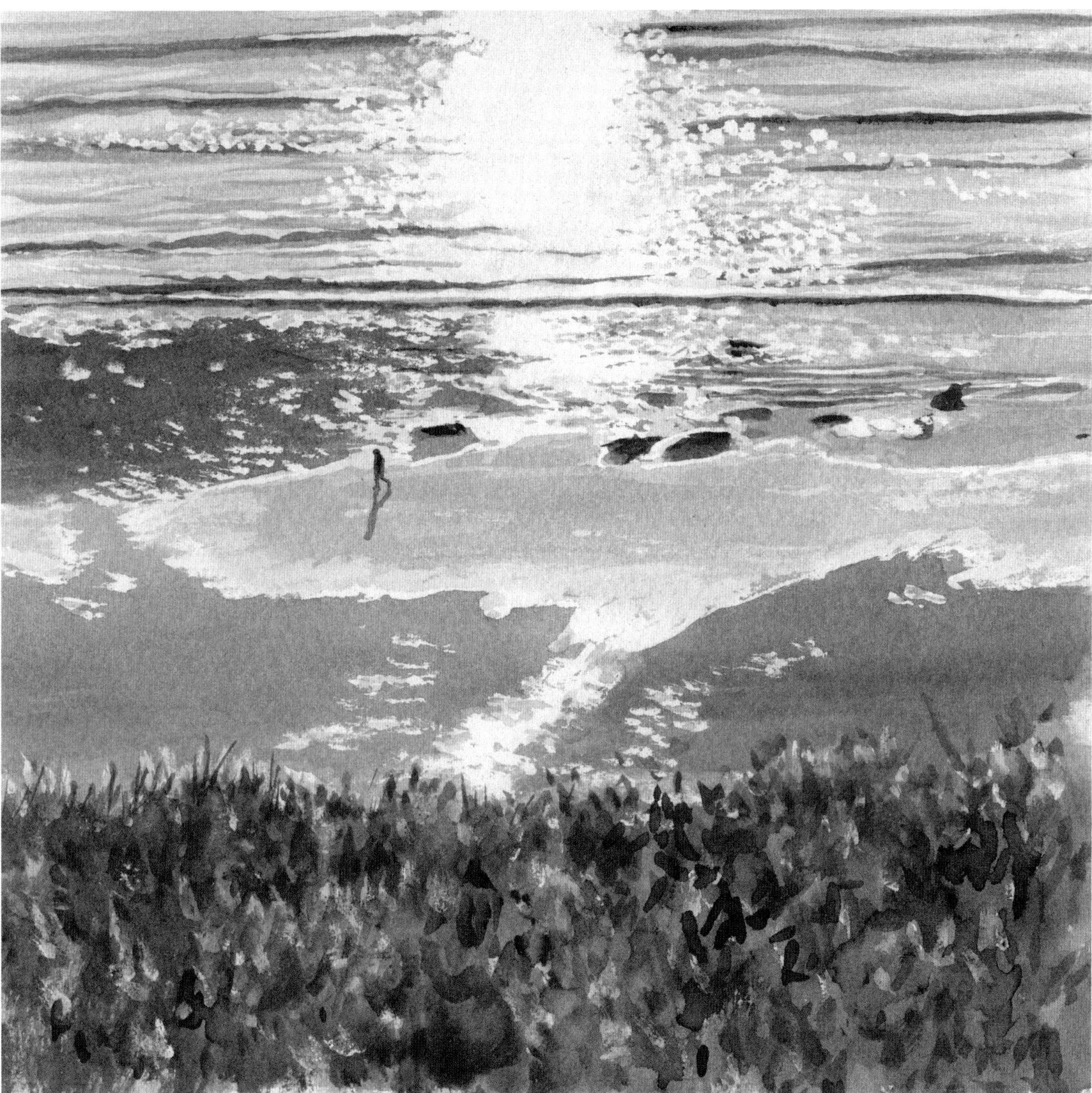

This Too Will Pass, 2023
Watercolour on paper, 20 x 20 cm (7 ⅞ x 7 ⅞ in.)

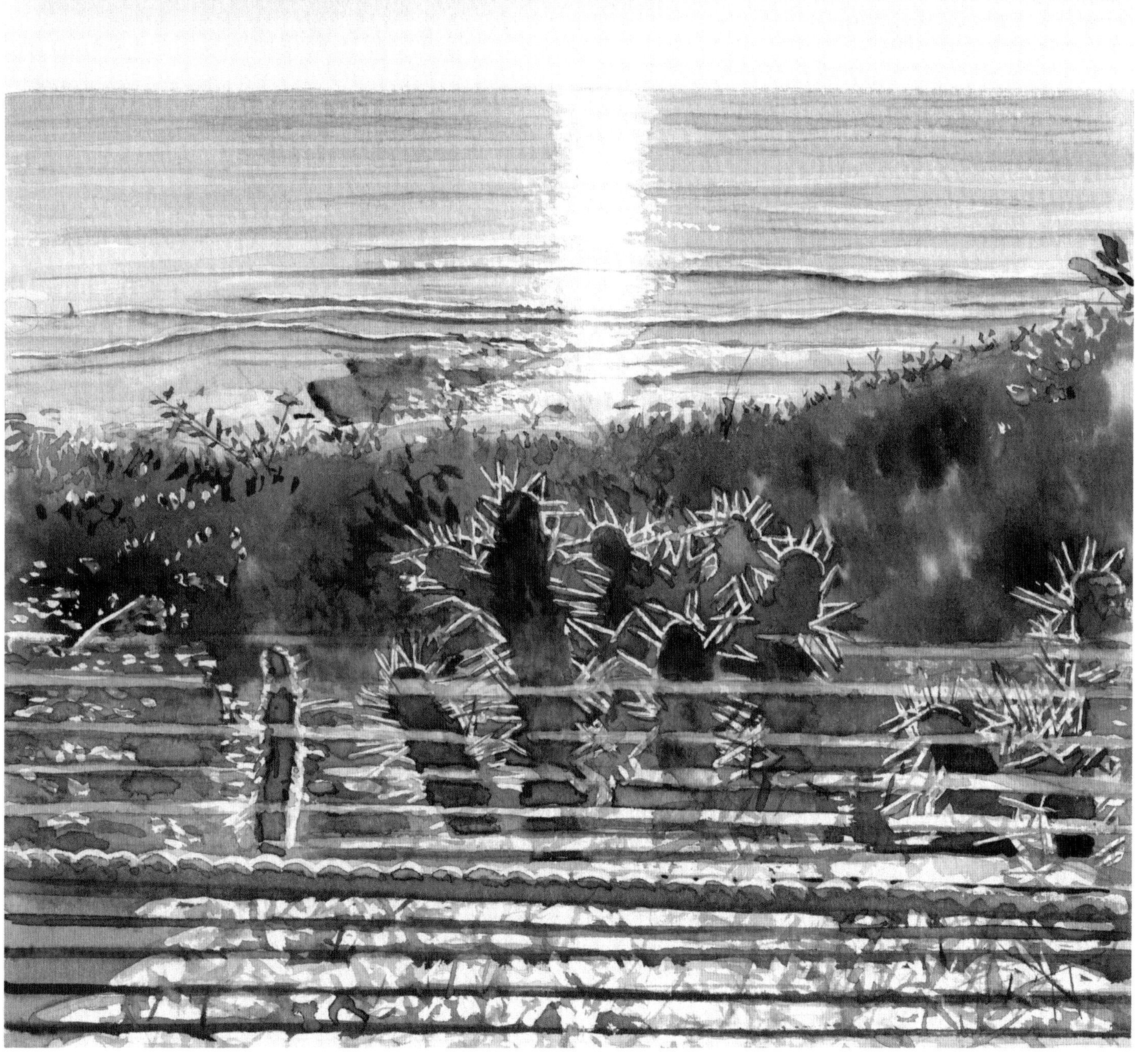

The Space Between Us, 2023
Watercolour on paper, 20 x 20 cm (7 ⅞ x 7 ⅞ in.)

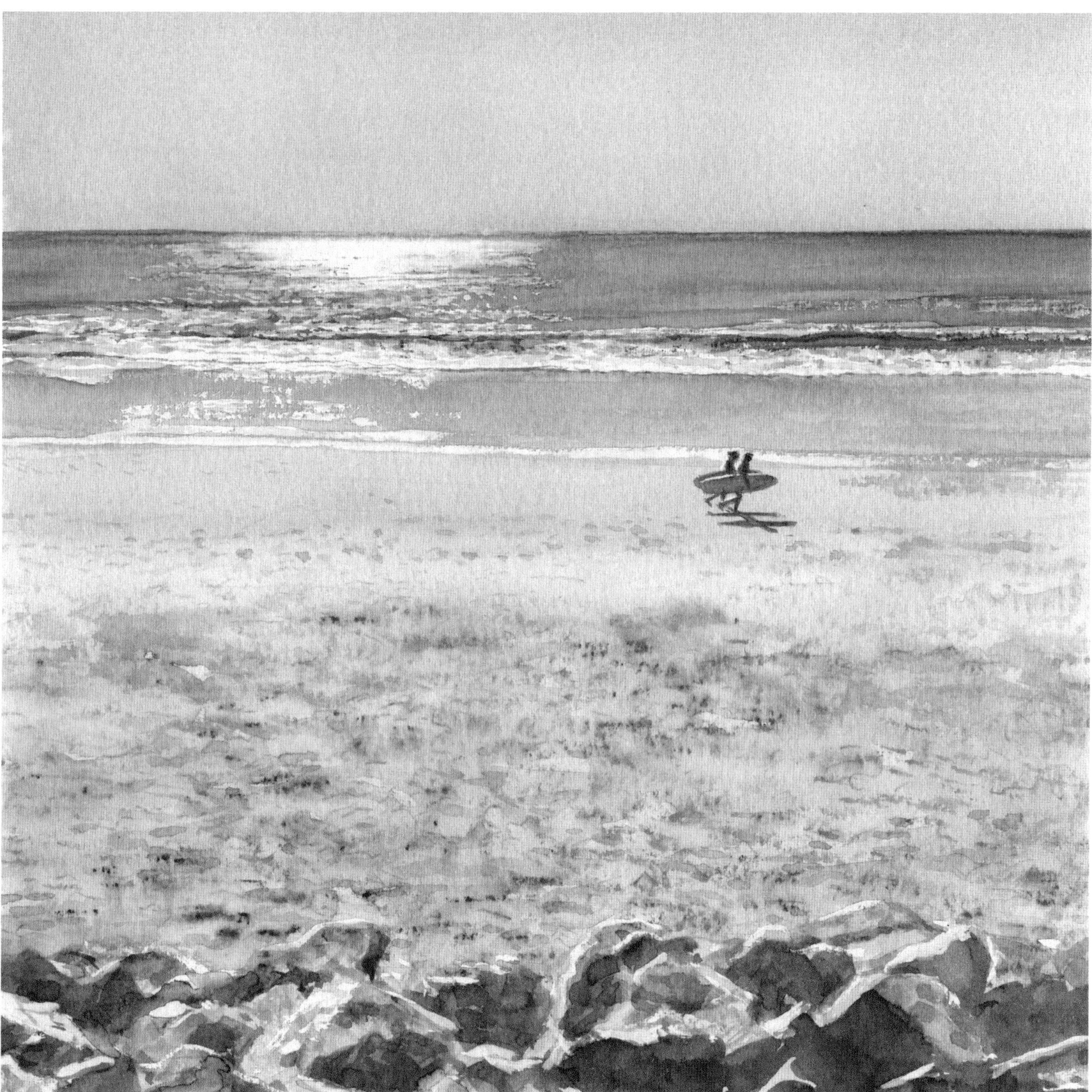

The Answer Is You, 2023
Watercolour on paper, 20 x 20 cm (7 ⅞ x 7 ⅞ in.)

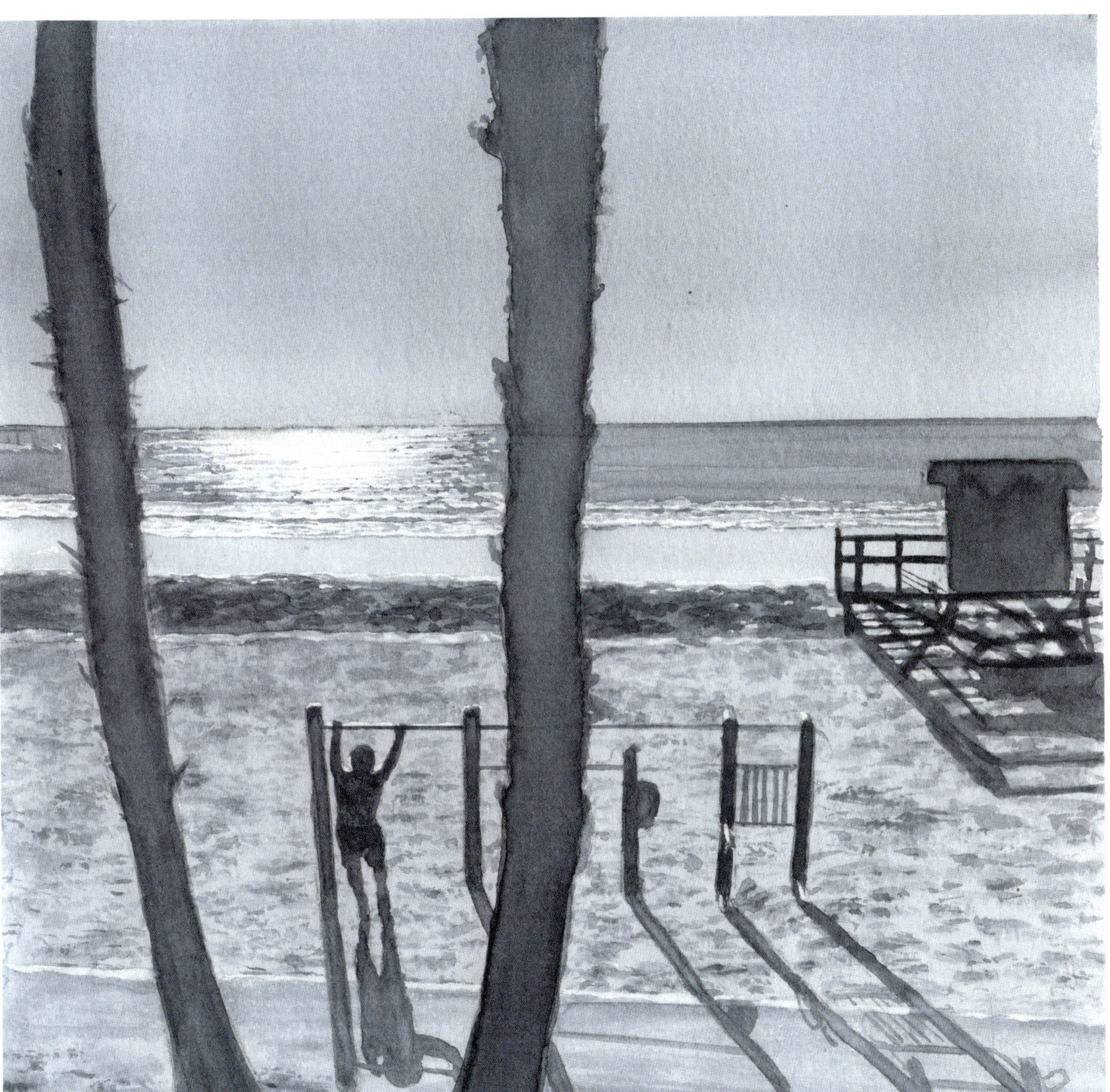

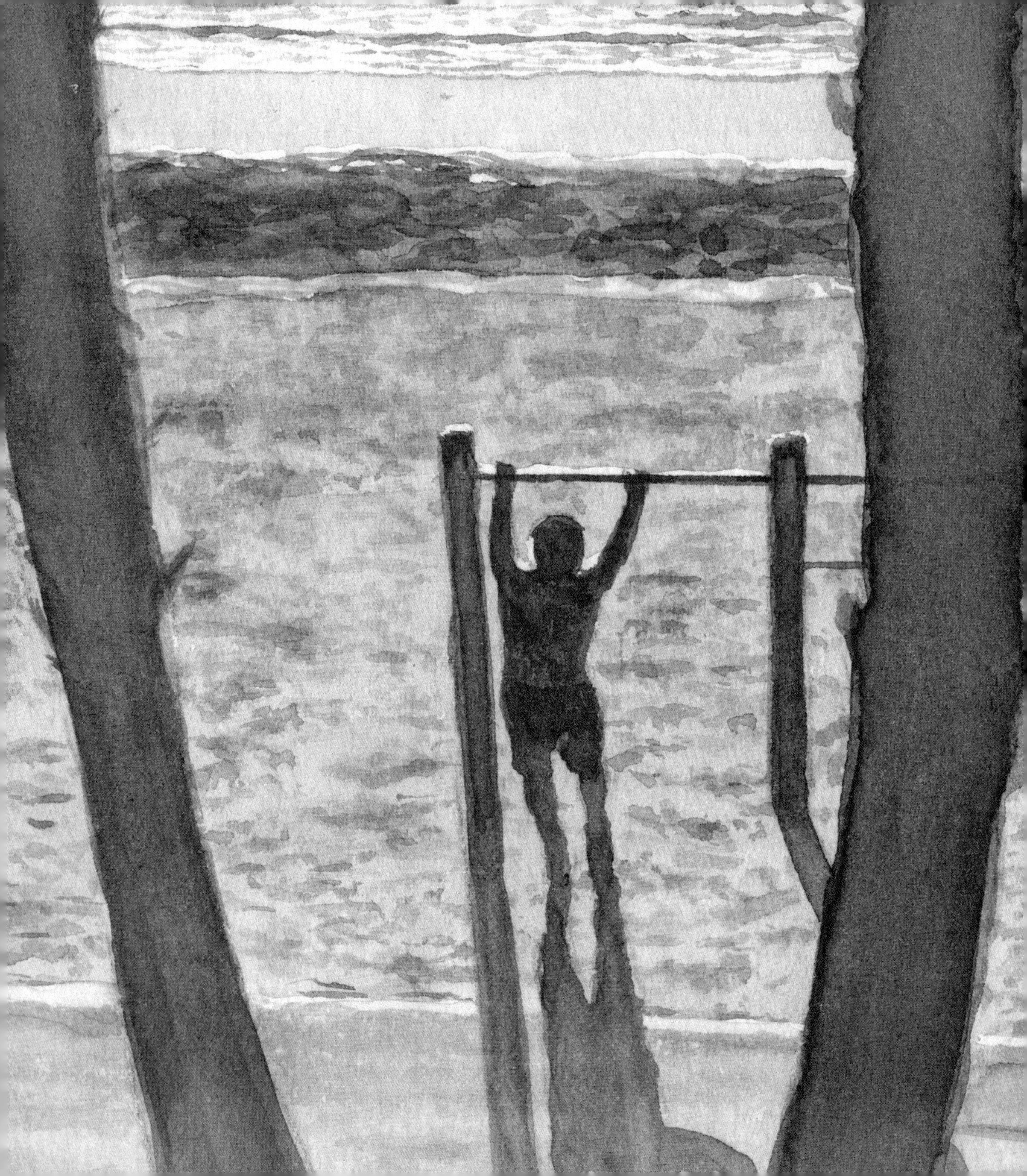

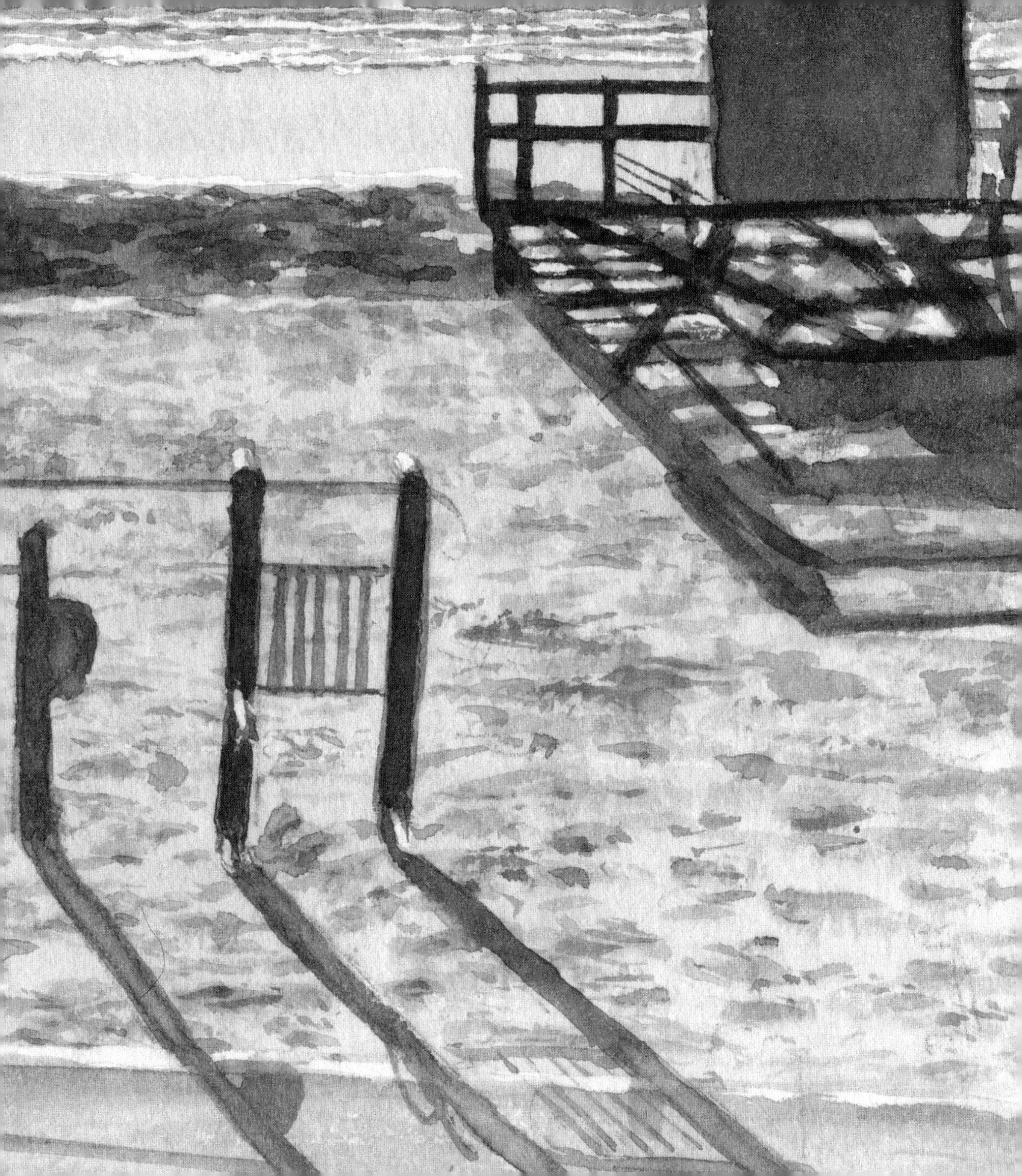

The Desert Had Turned to Sea, 2023
Watercolour on paper, 20 x 20 cm (7 ⅞ x 7 ⅞ in.)

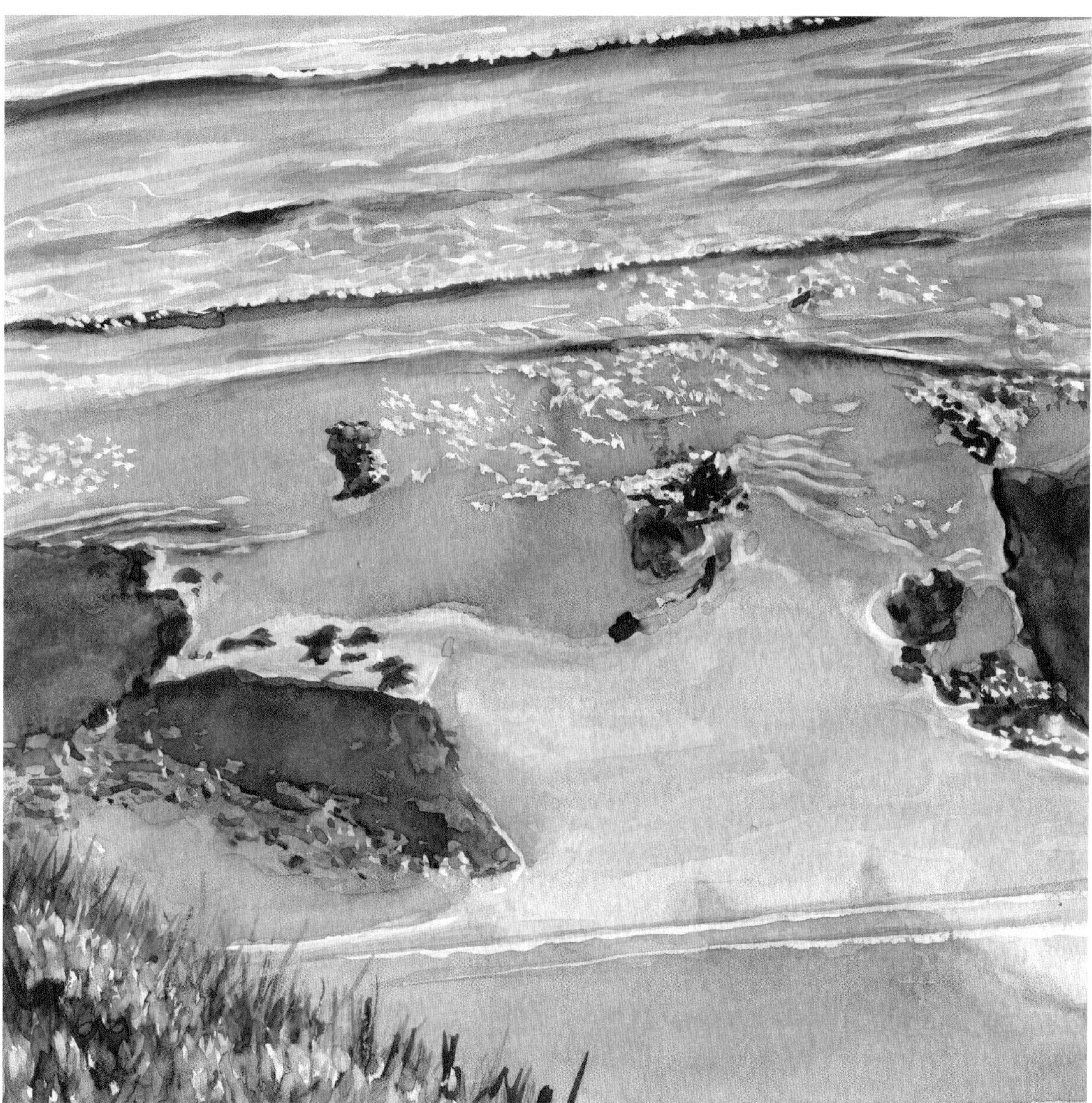

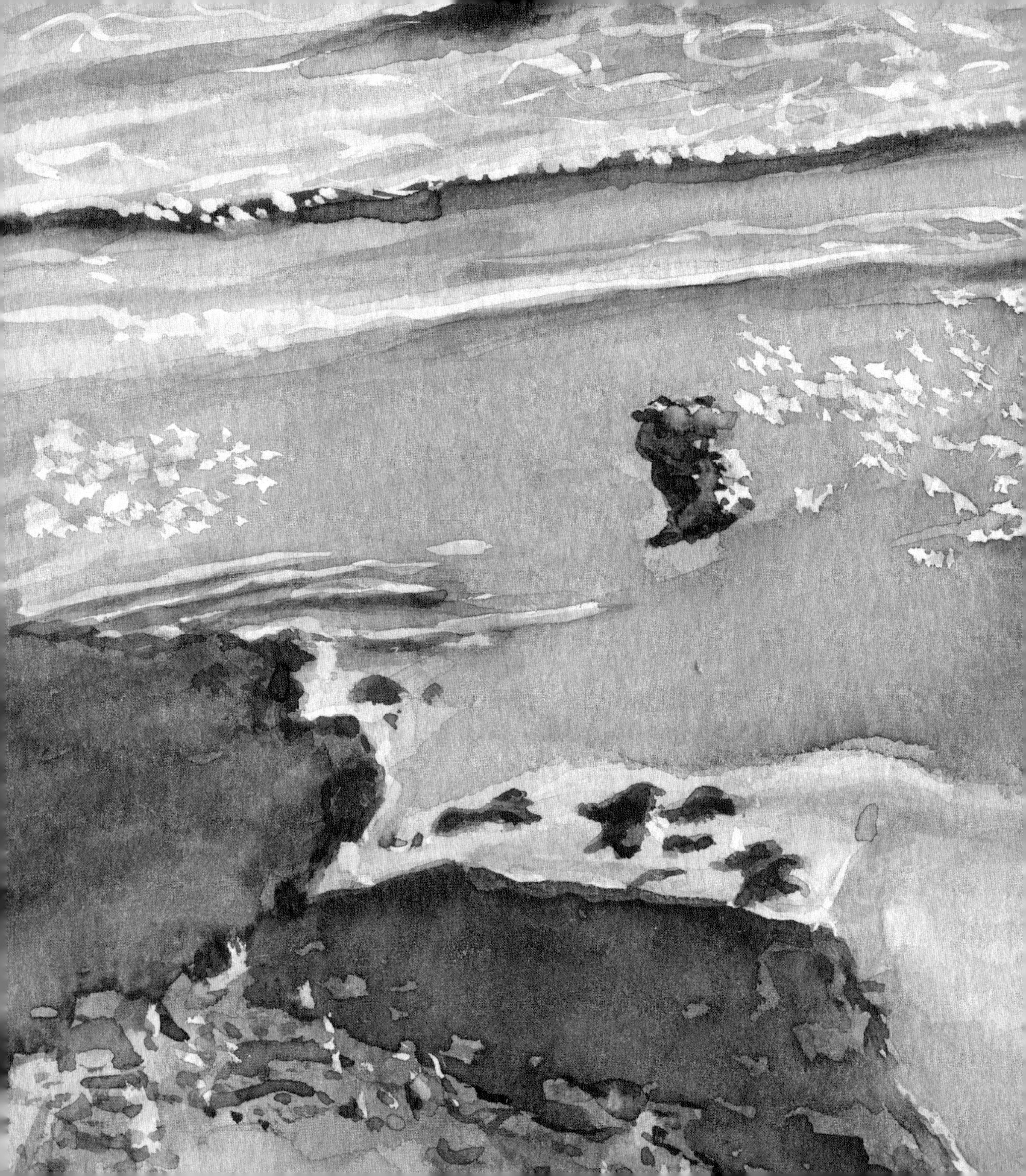

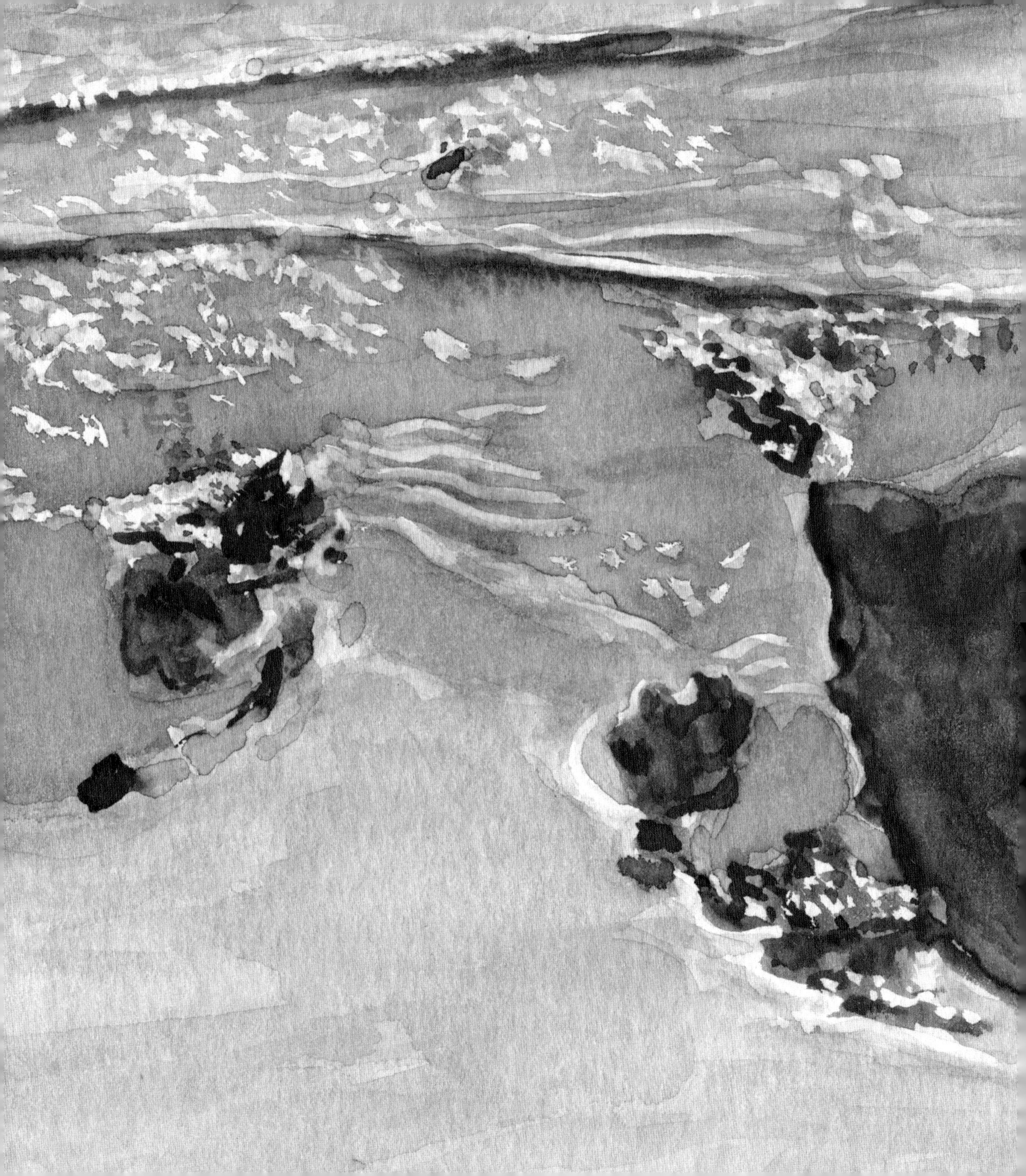

Wholly Other, 2023
Watercolour on paper, 20 x 20 cm (7 ⅞ x 7 ⅞ in.)

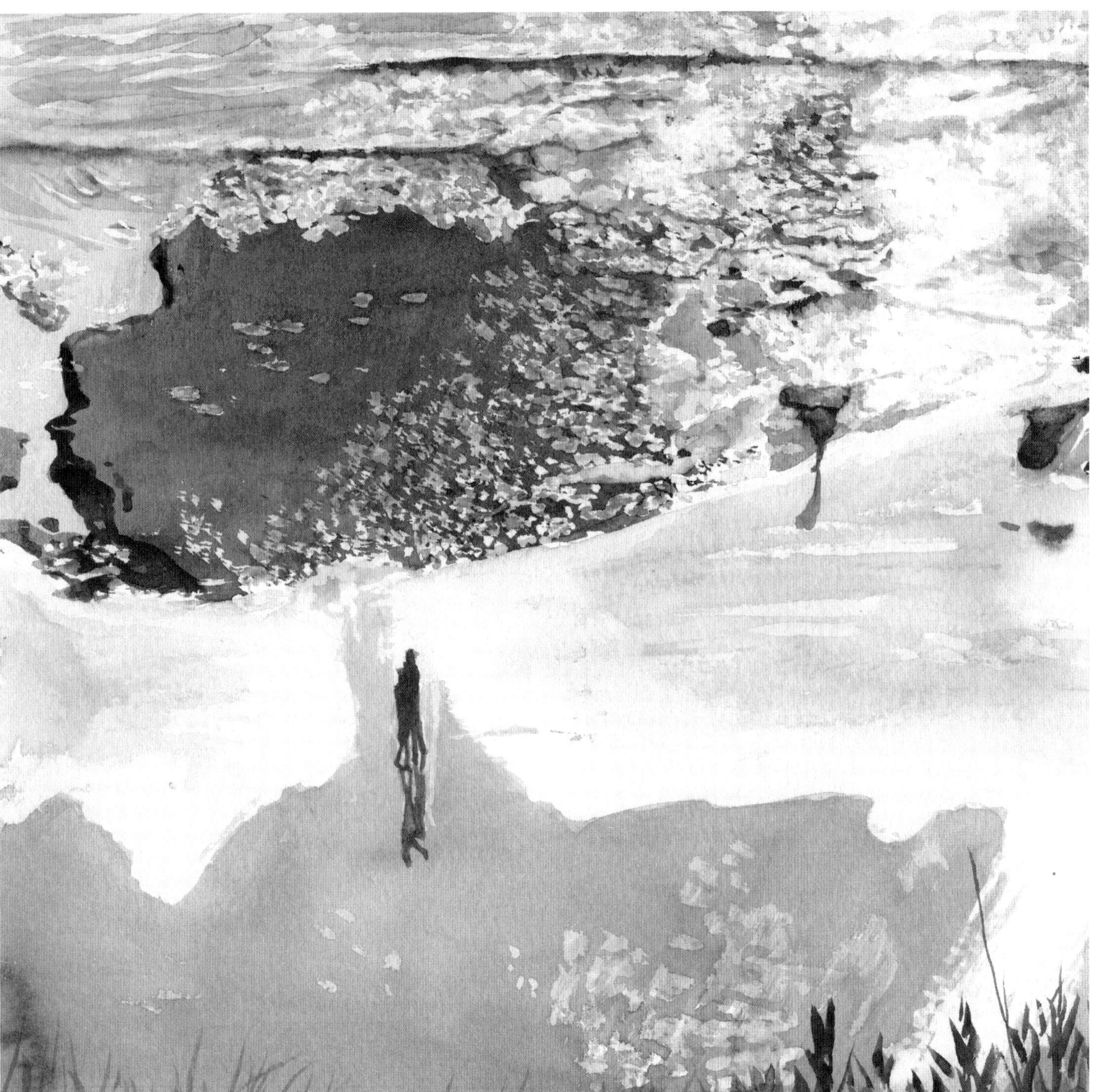

Burst of Illumination, 2023
Watercolour on paper, 20 x 20 cm (7 ⅞ x 7 ⅞ in.)

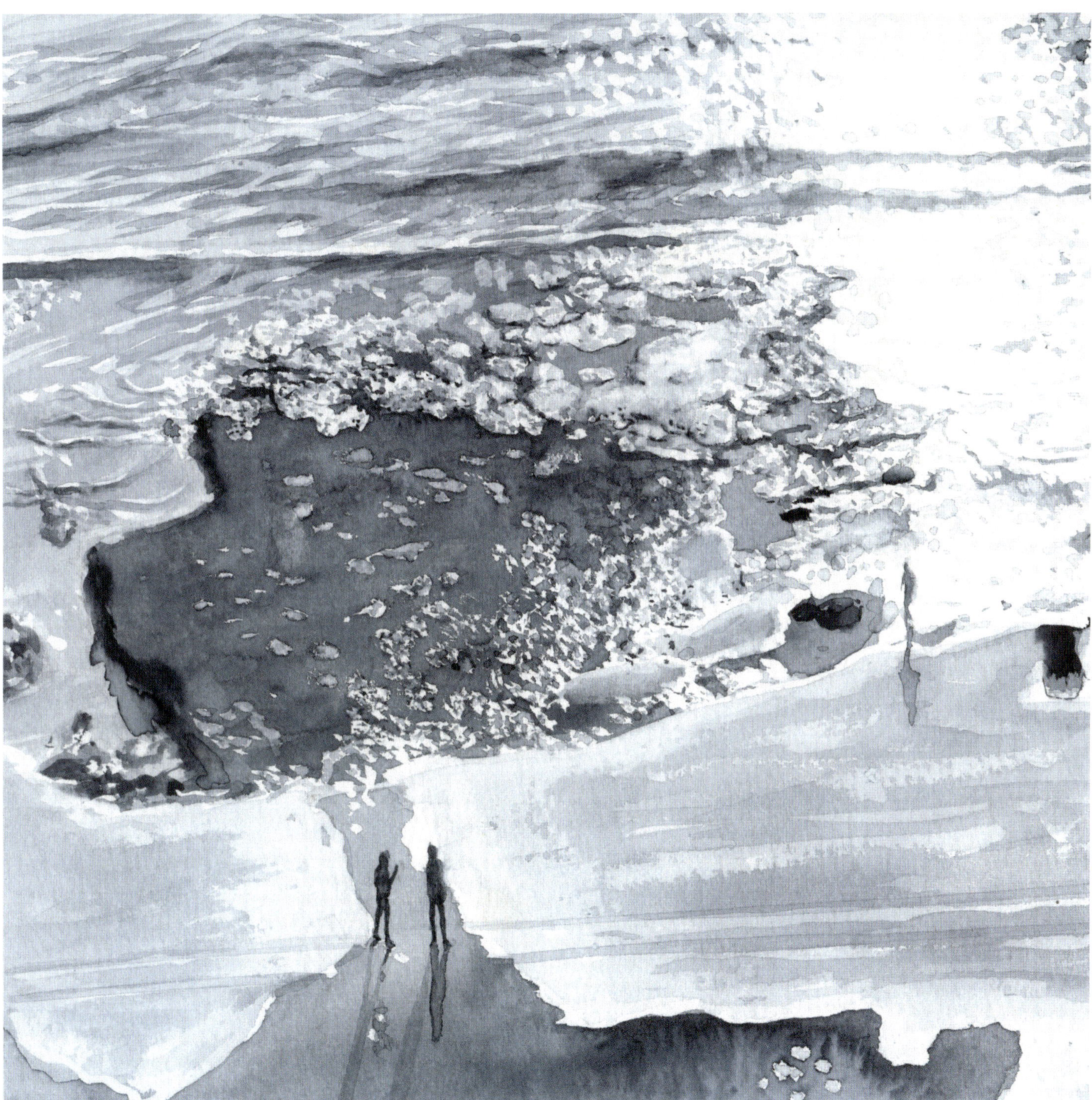

Mystery and Marvel, 2023
Watercolour on paper, 20 x 20 cm (7 ⅞ x 7 ⅞ in.)

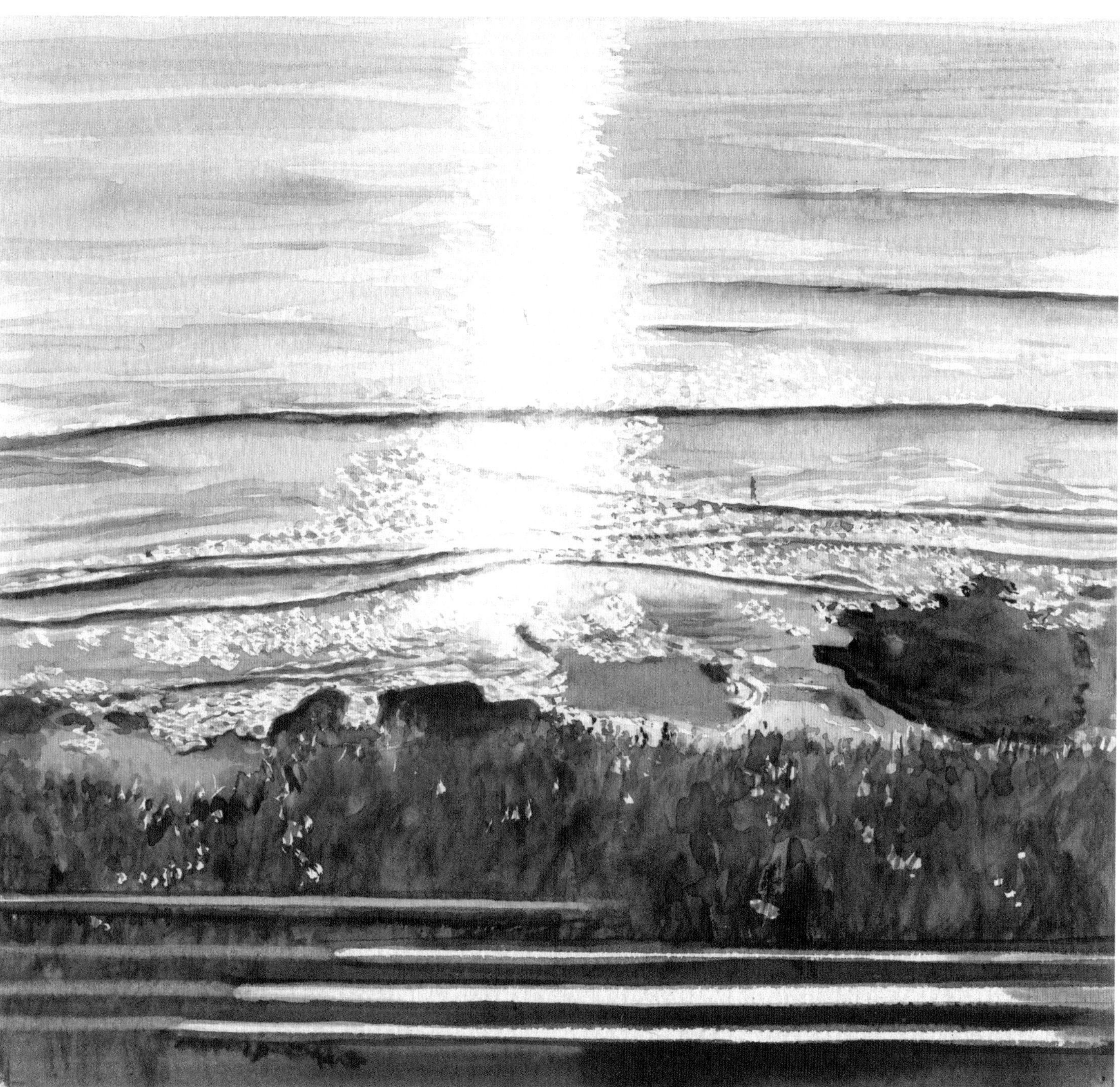

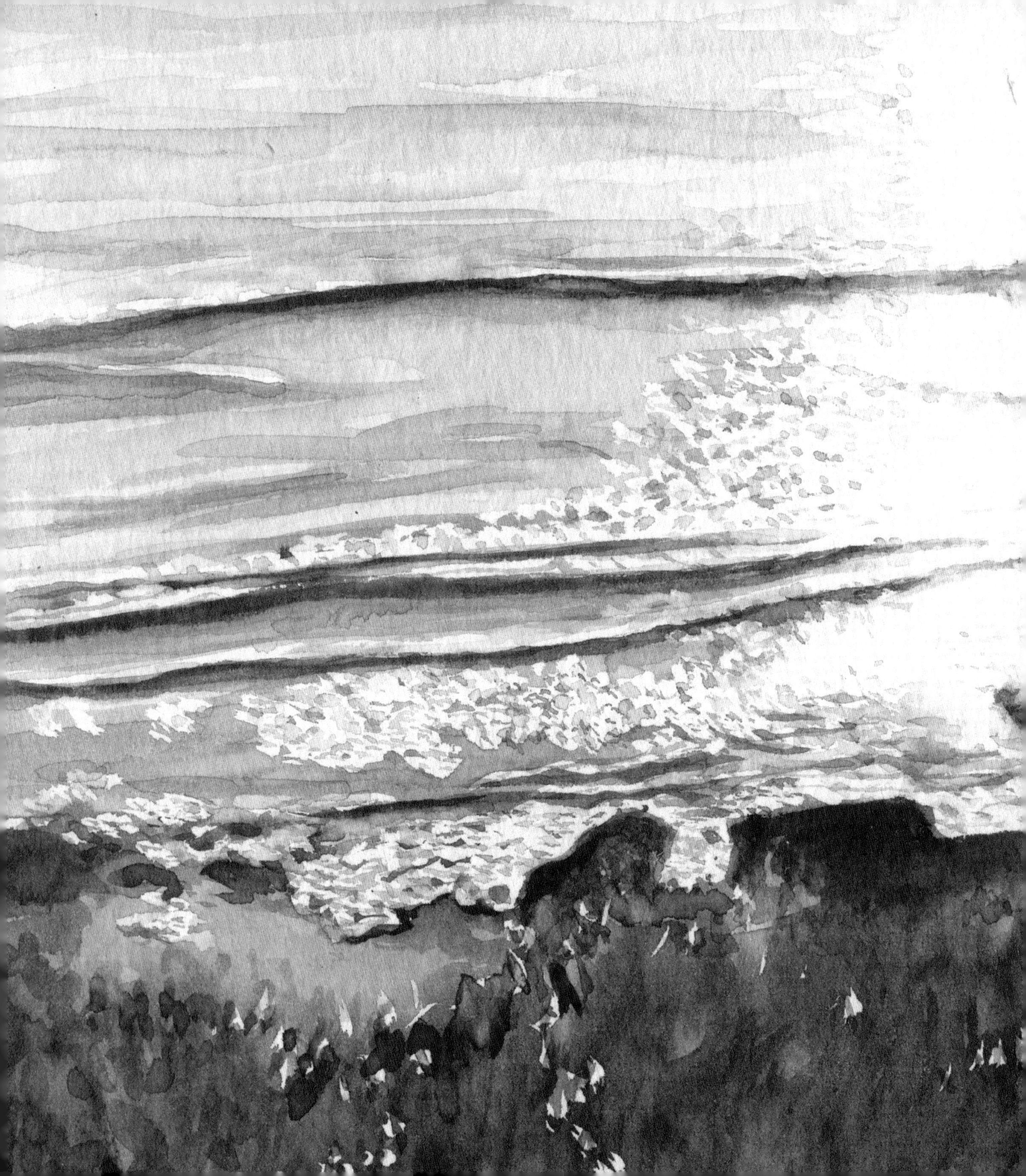

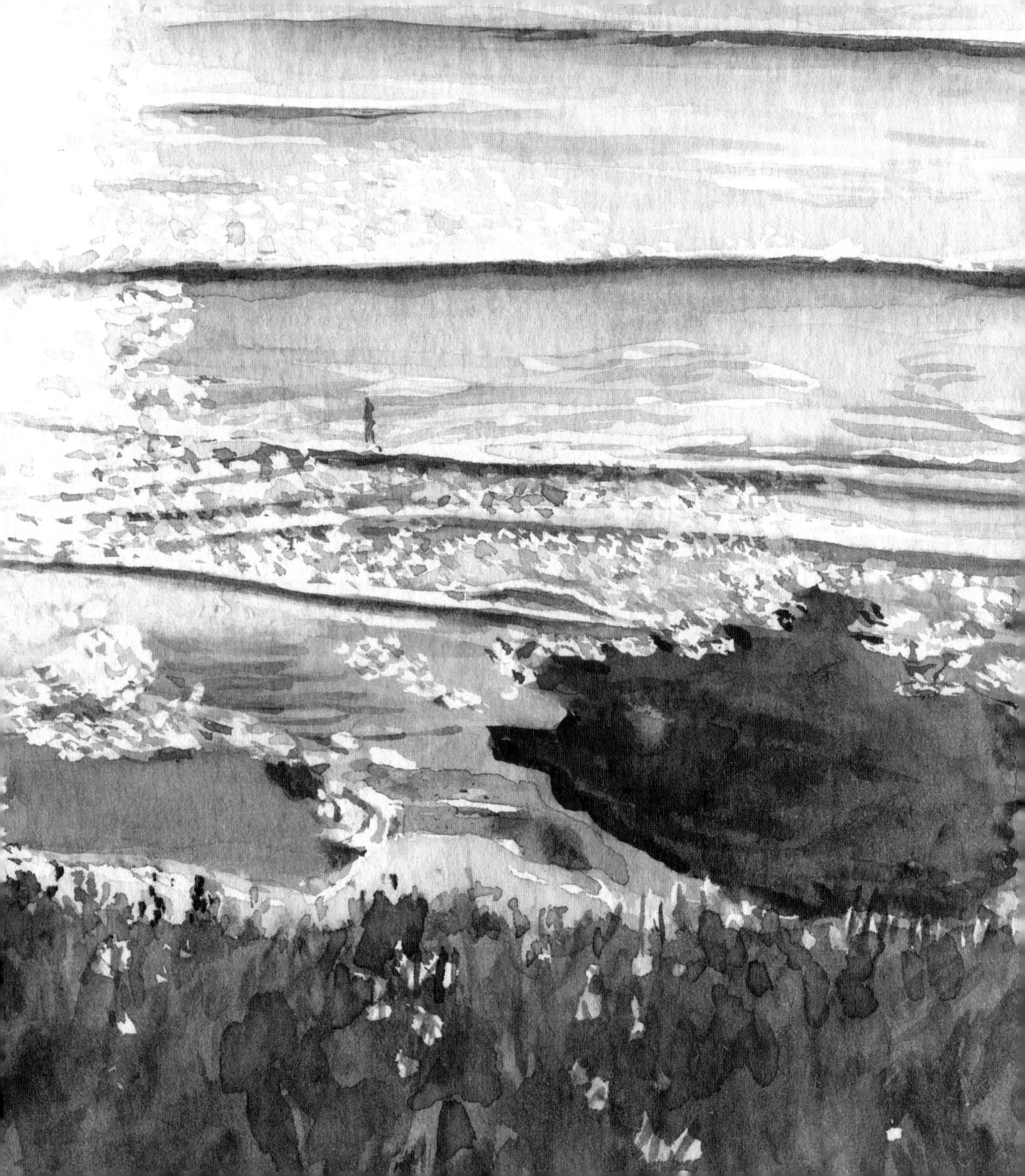

Diamonds Dancing on Water, 2023
Watercolour on paper, 20 x 20 cm (7 ⅞ x 7 ⅞ in.)

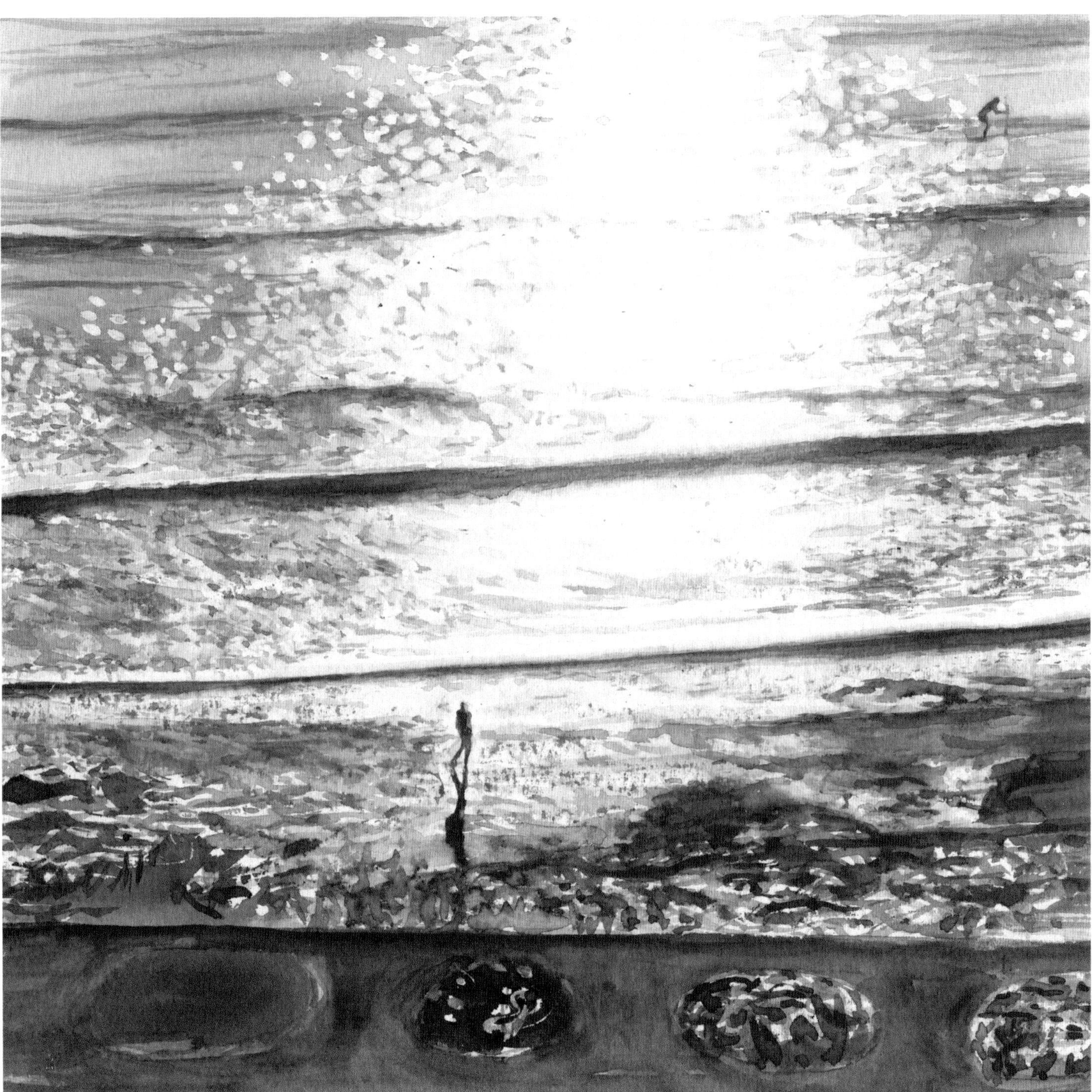

Throw Those Curtains Wide, 2023
Watercolour on paper, 20 x 20 cm (7 ⅞ x 7 ⅞ in.)

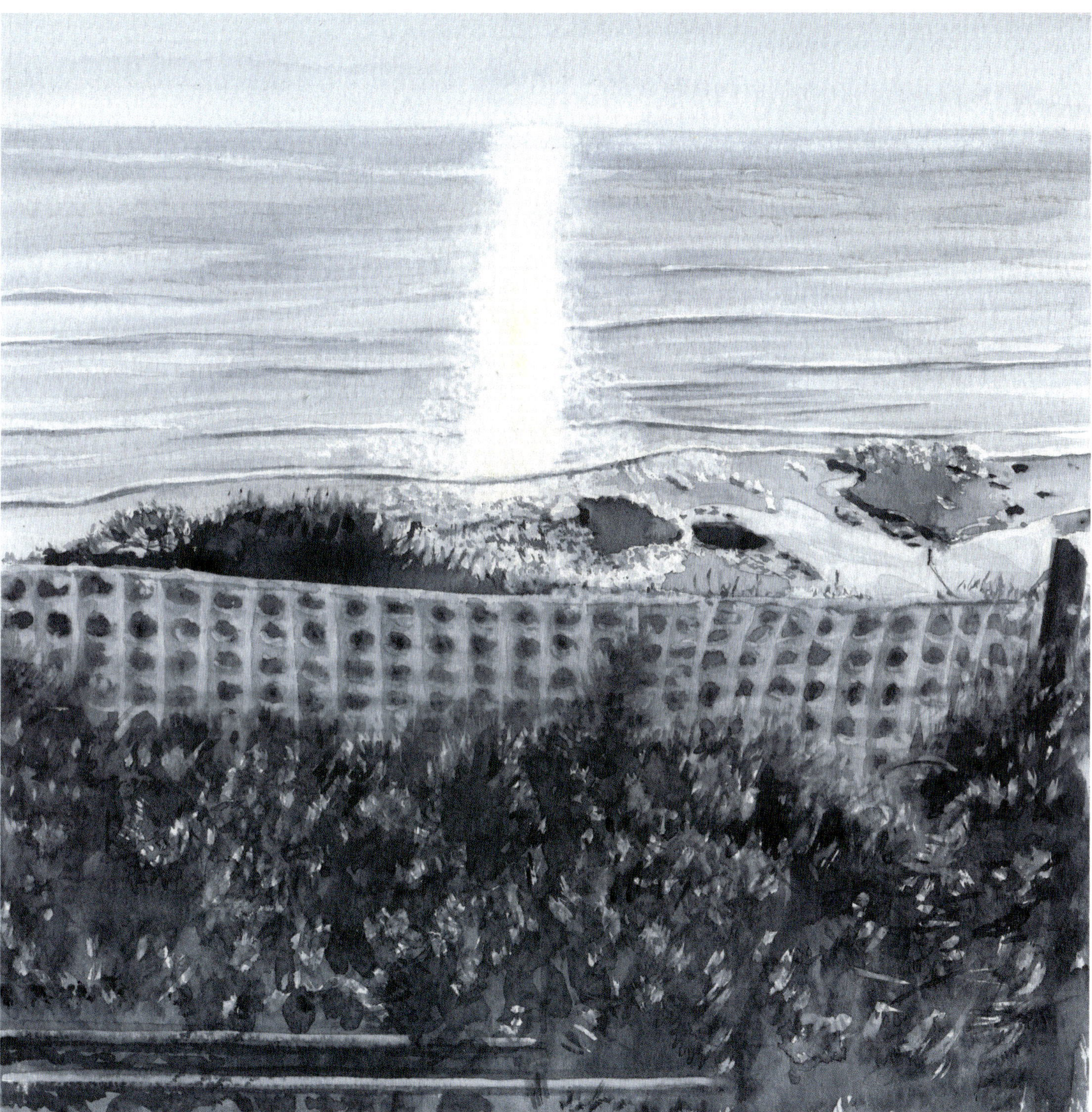

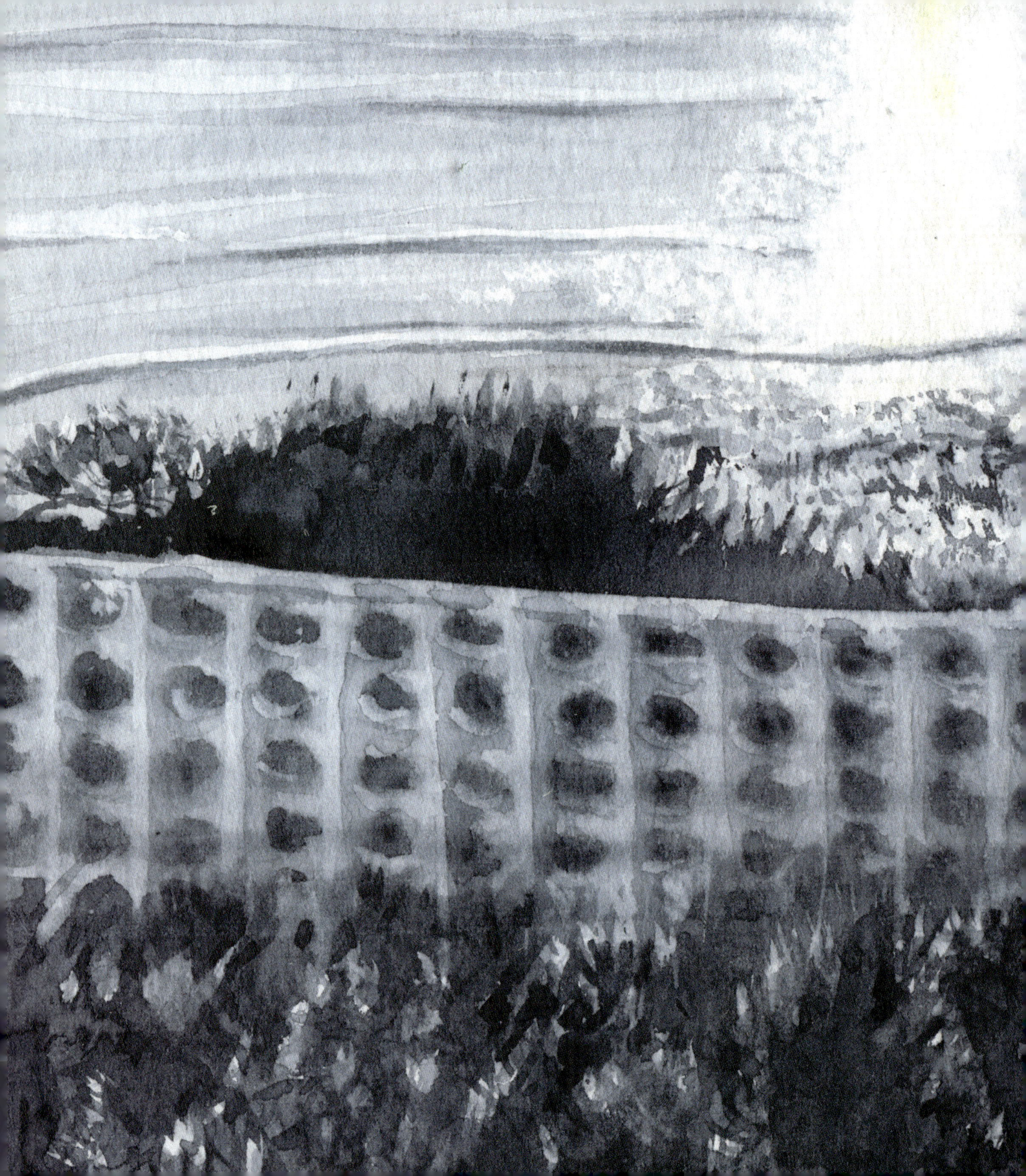

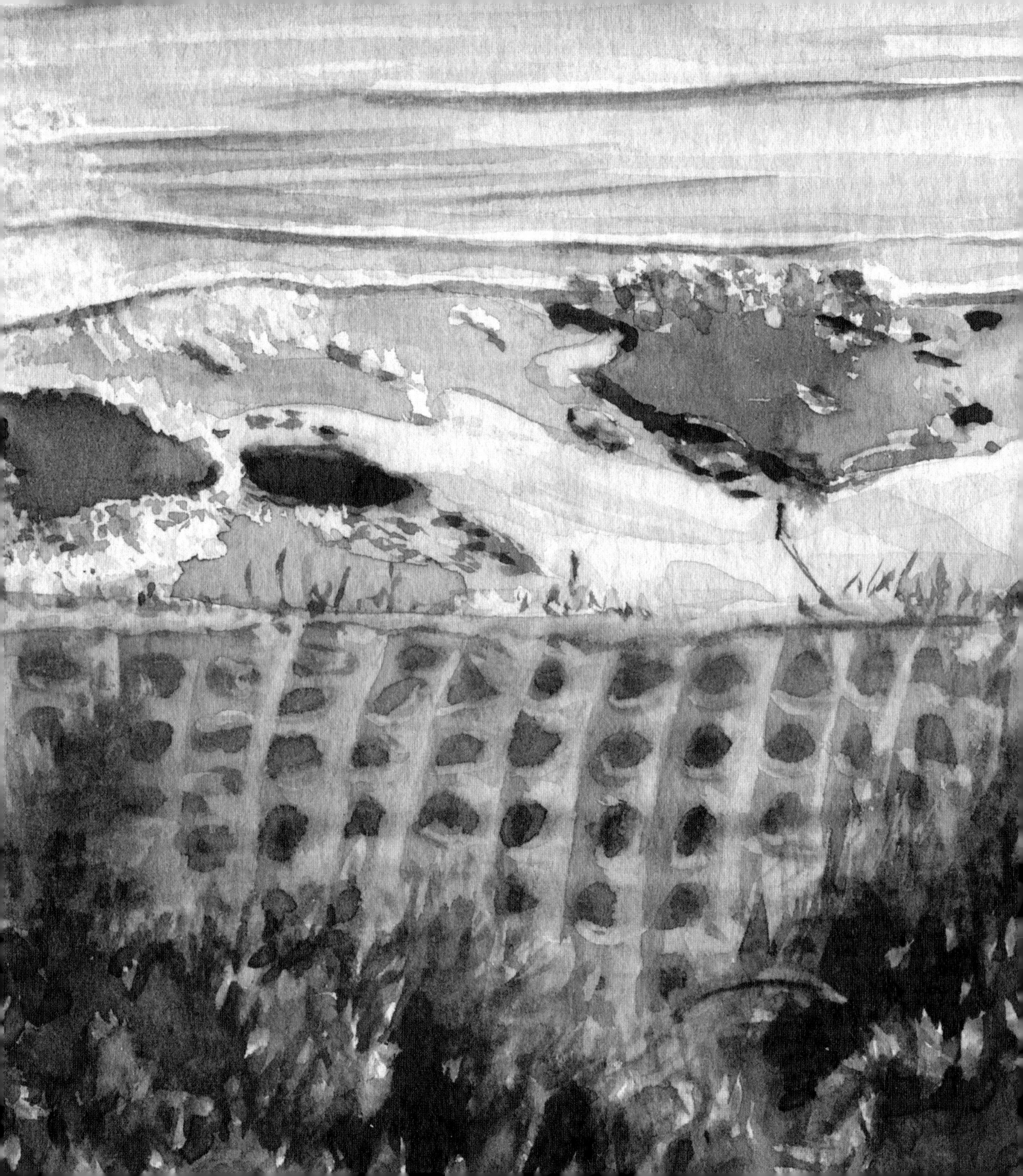

Transcends Reason and Thought, 2023
Watercolour on paper, 20 x 20 cm (7 ⅞ x 7 ⅞ in.)

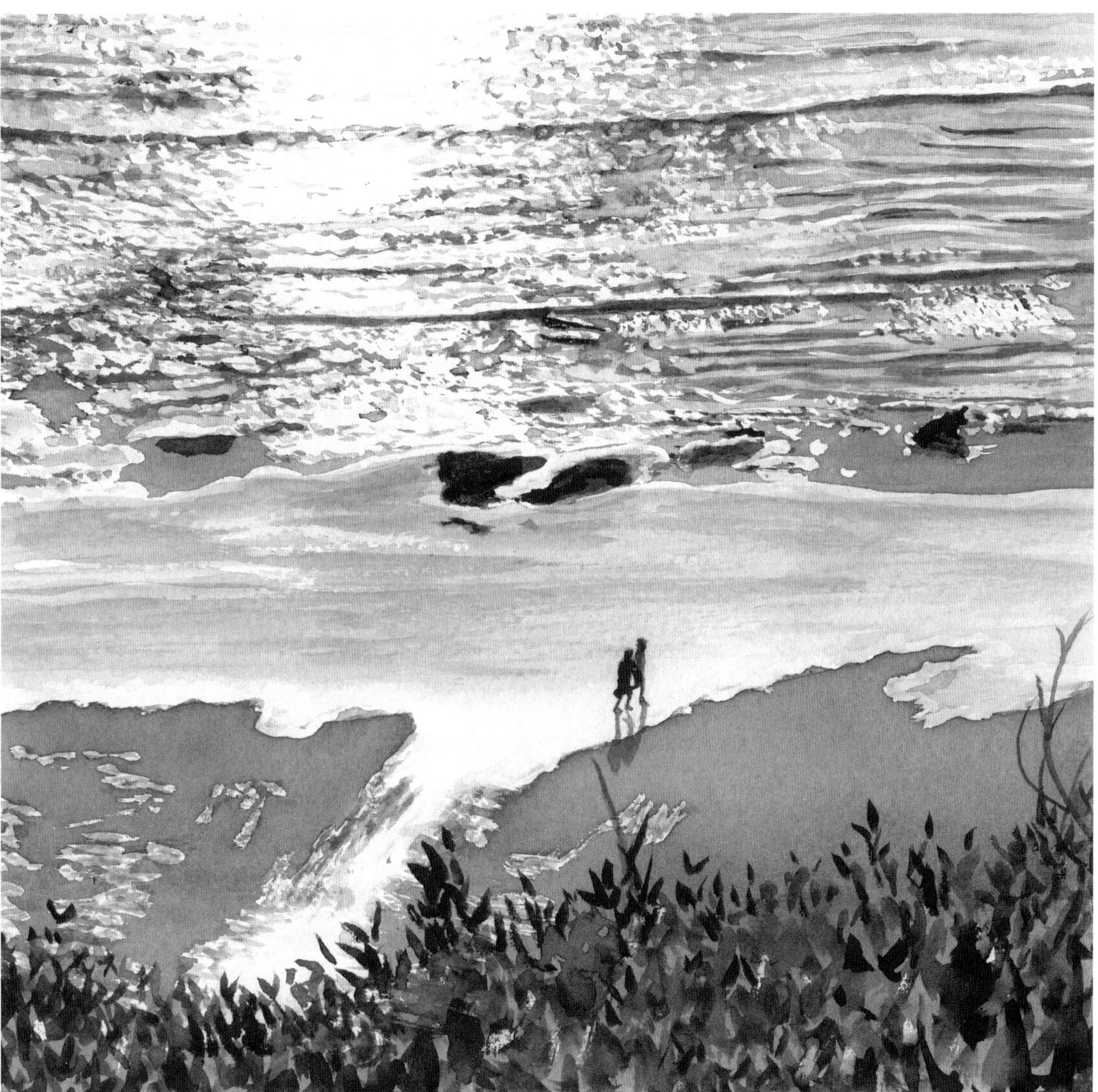

Wonder in the Wonder, 2023
Watercolour on paper, 20 x 20 cm (7 ⅛ x 7 ⅛ in.)

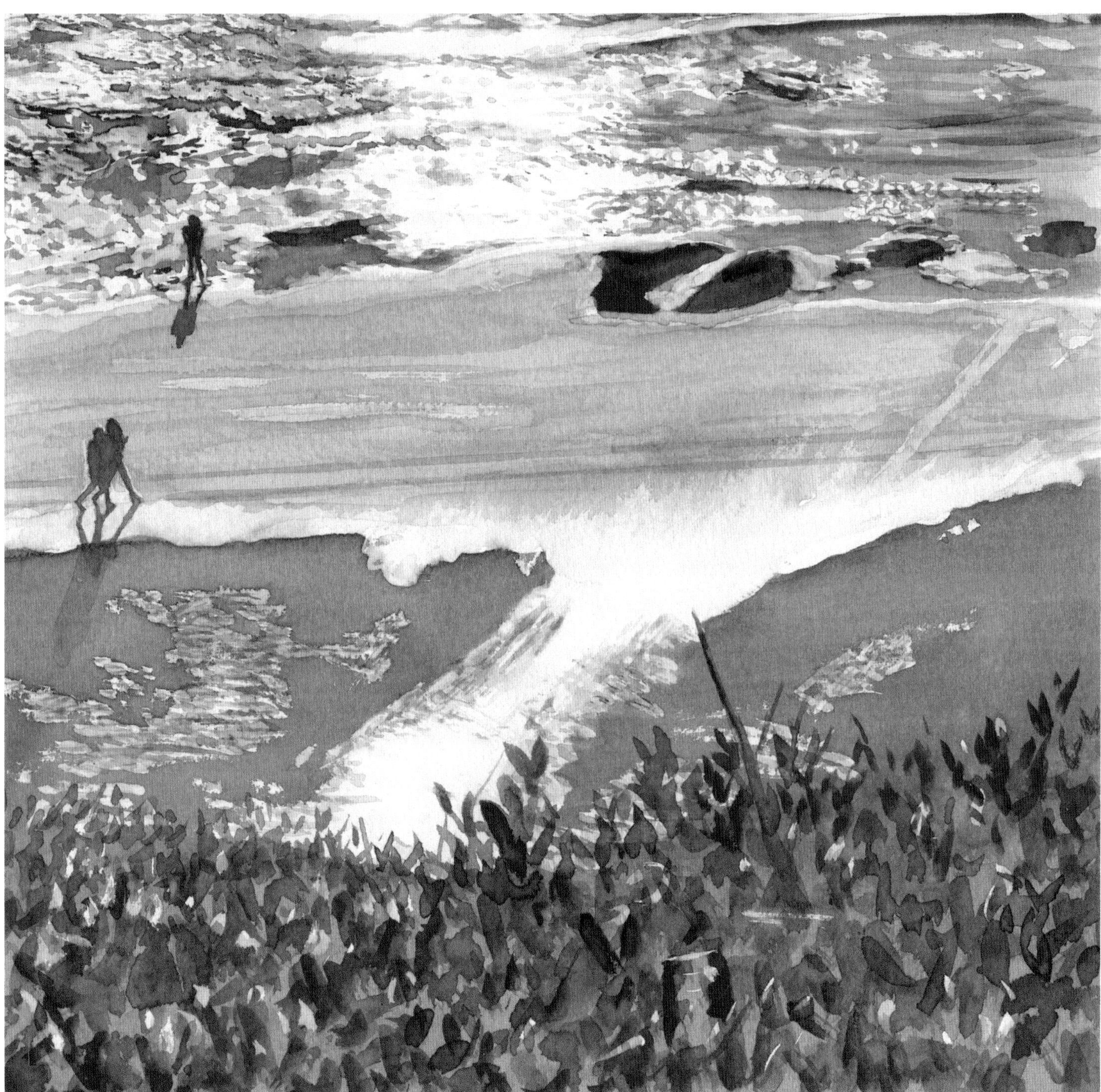

The Air Was Full of Silence, 2023
Watercolour on paper, 20 x 20 cm (7 ⅞ x 7 ⅞ in.)

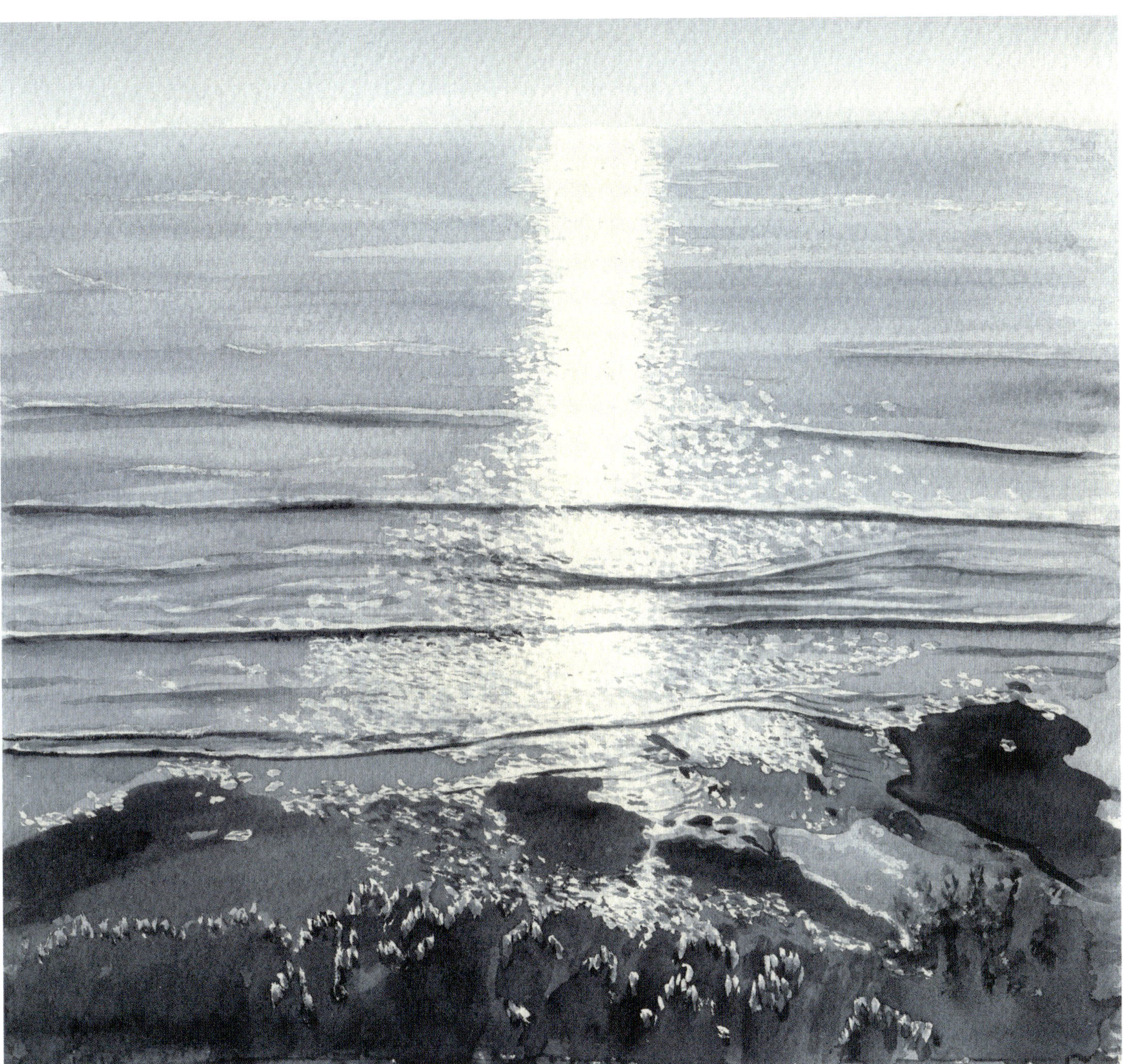

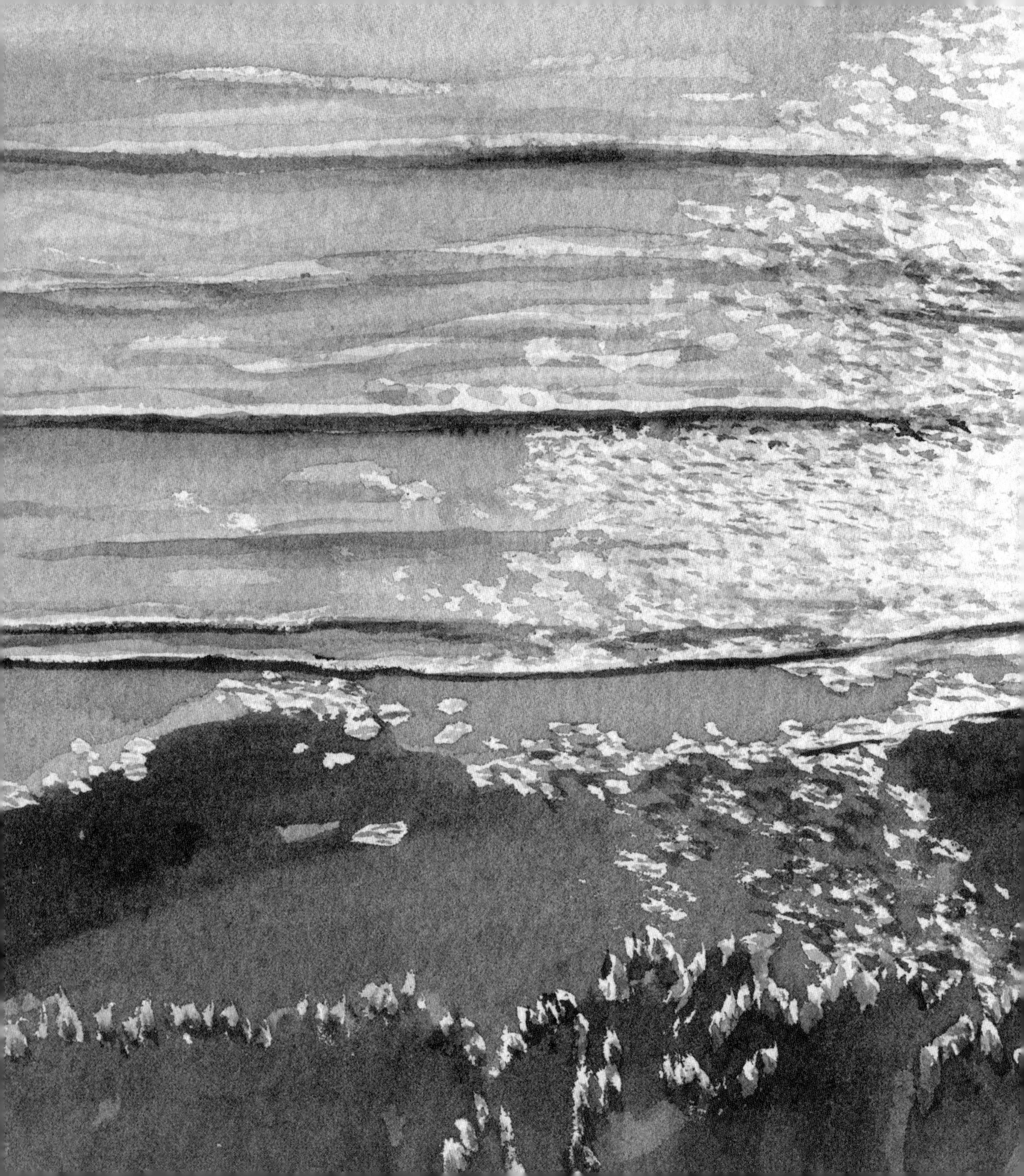

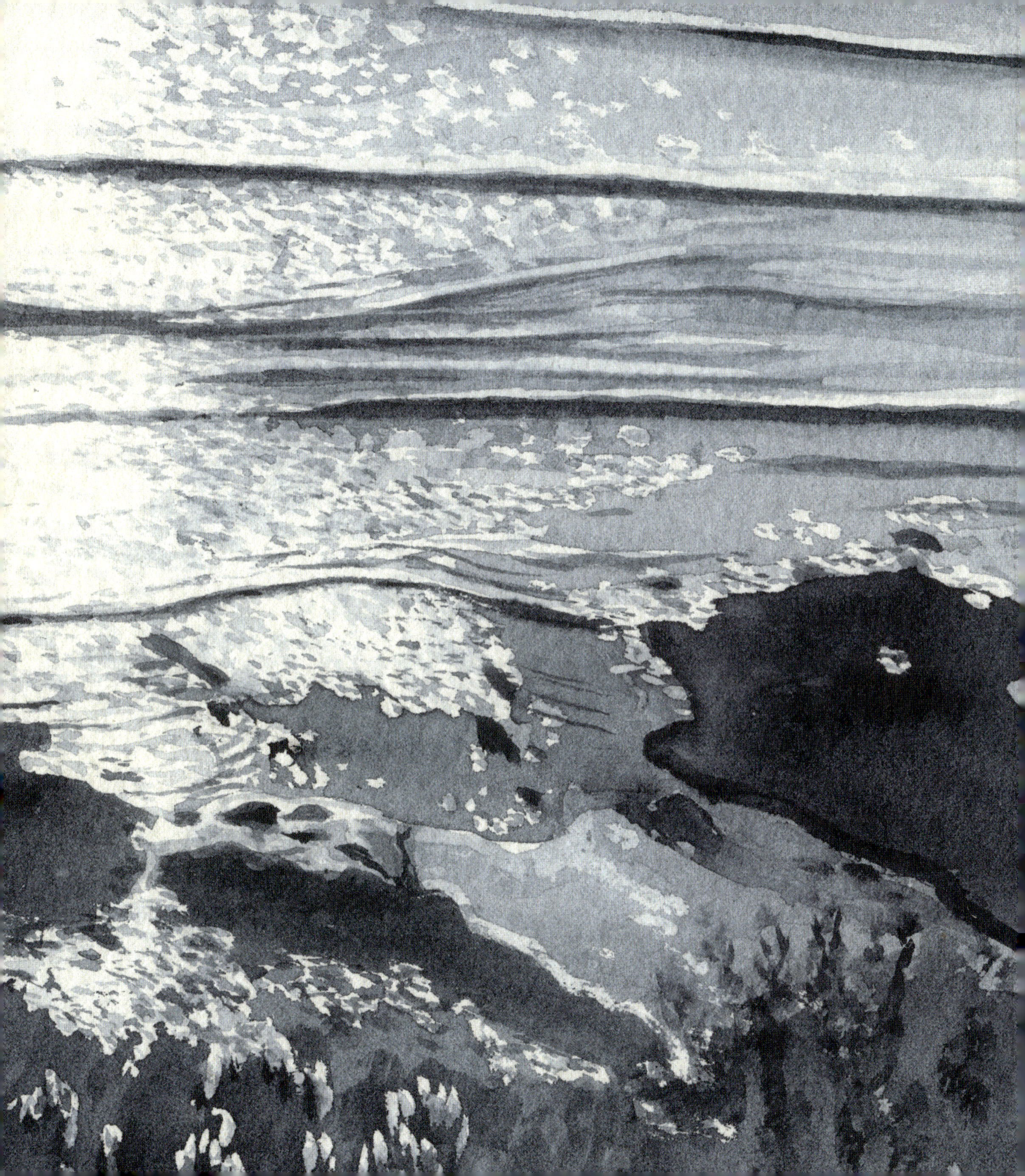

Look for the Light, 2023
Watercolour on paper, 20 x 20 cm (7 ⅞ x 7 ⅞ in.)

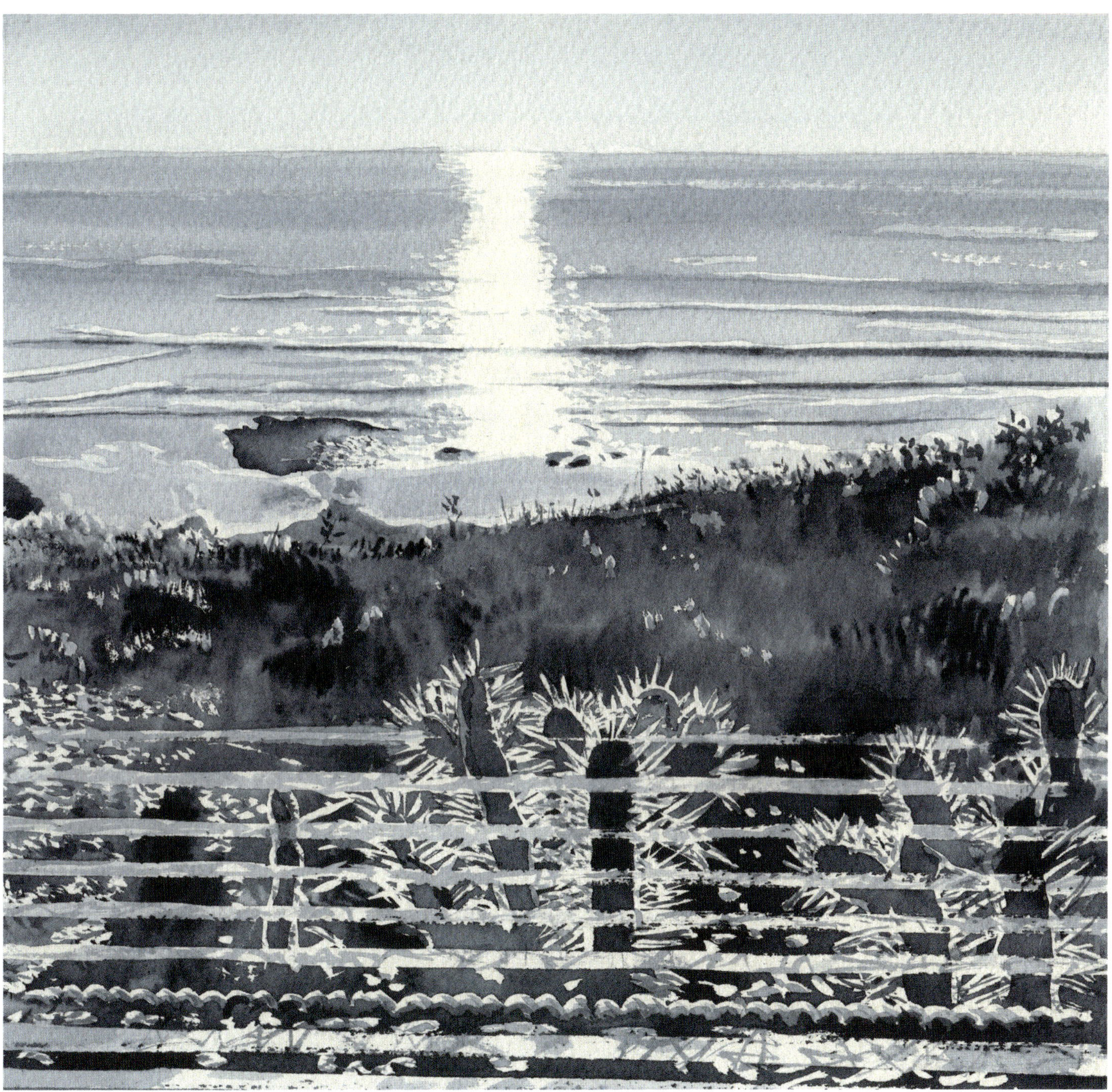

Honour by Silence, 2023
Watercolour on paper, 20 x 20 cm (7 ⅞ x 7 ⅞ in.)

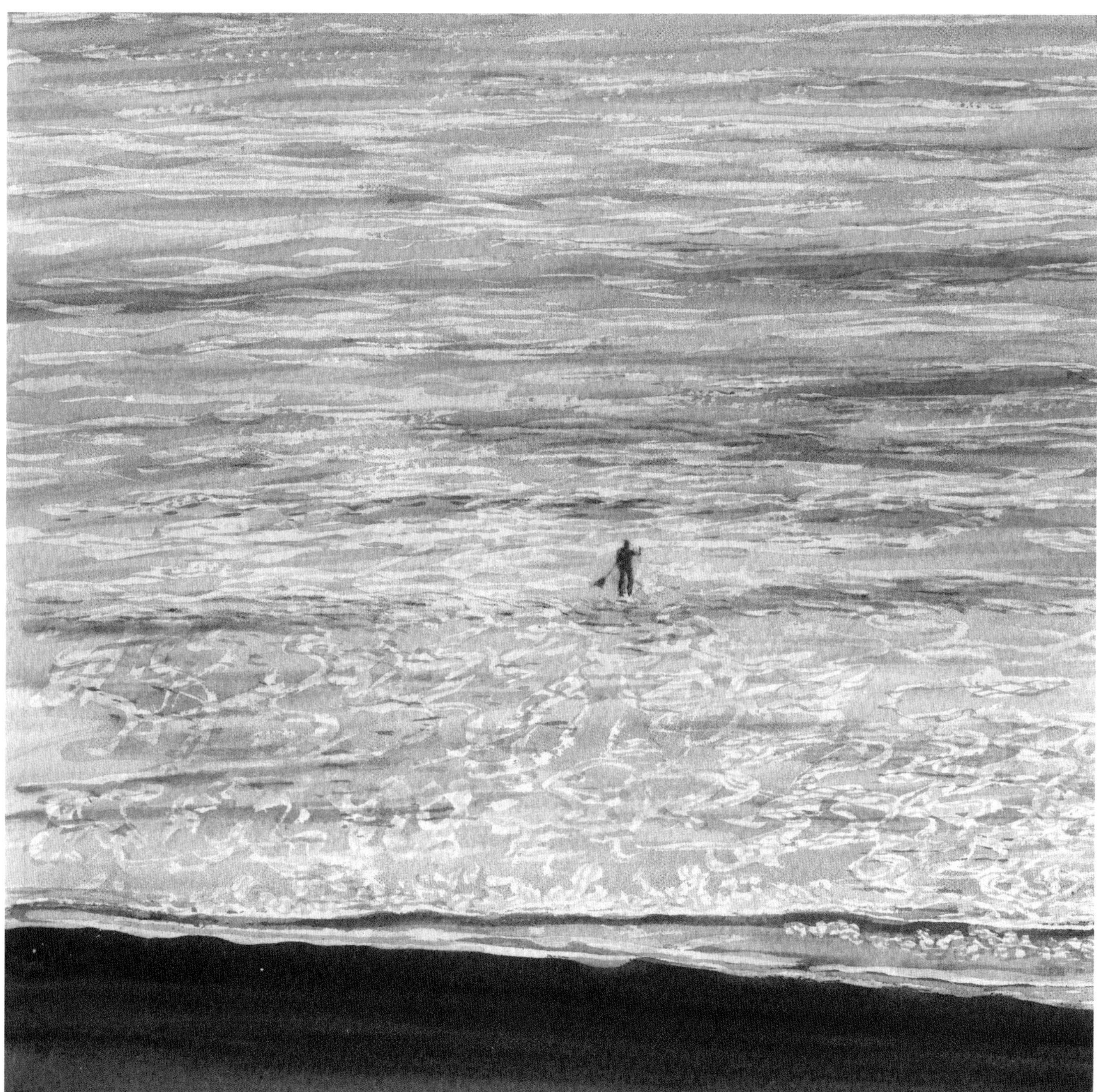

Refuge of the Roads, 2023
Oil on canvas, 100 x 100 cm (39 ⅜ x 39 ⅜ in.)

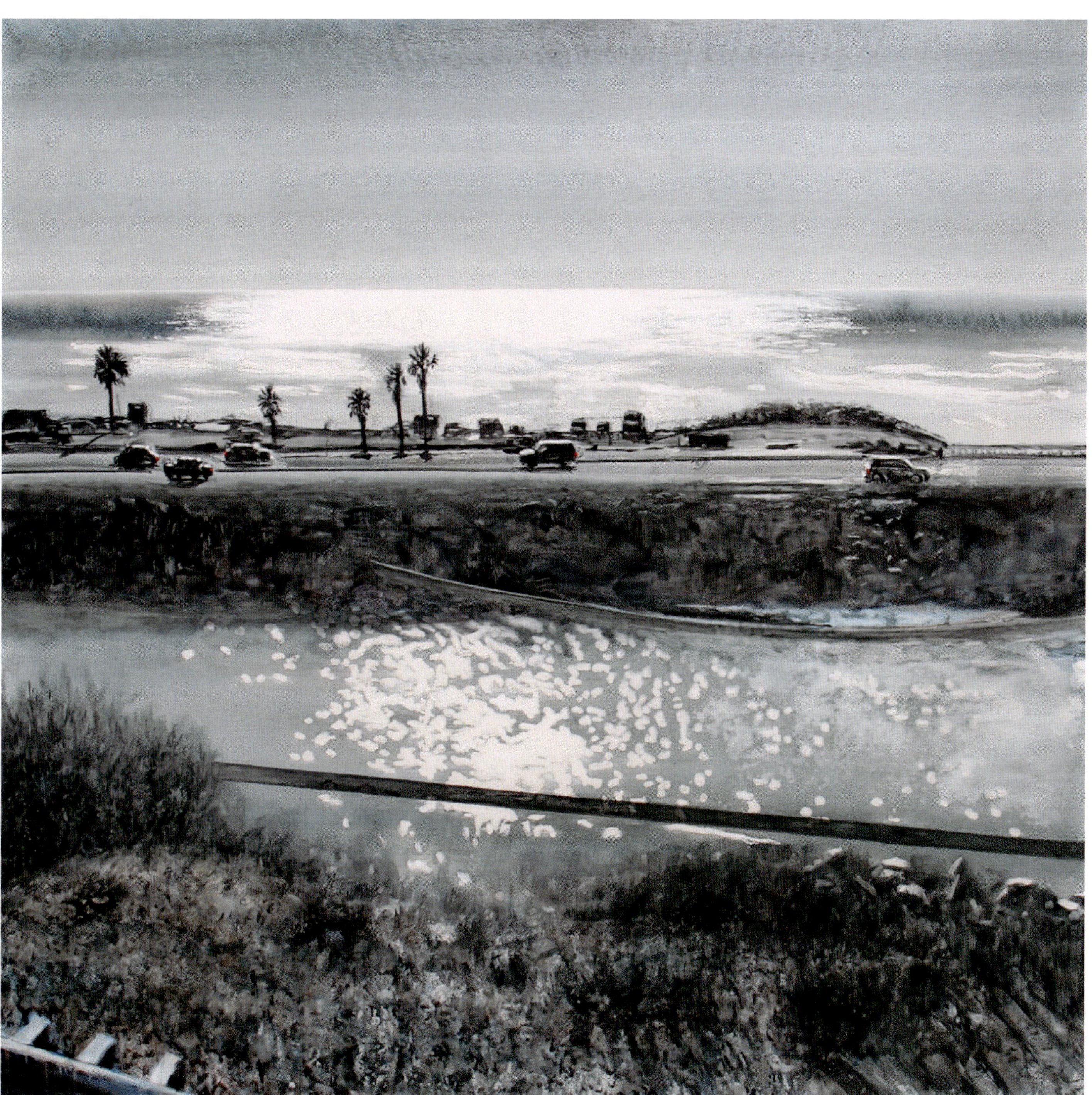

I Fell into the Water, 2023
Oil on canvas, 100 x 100 cm (39 ⅜ x 39 ⅜ in.)

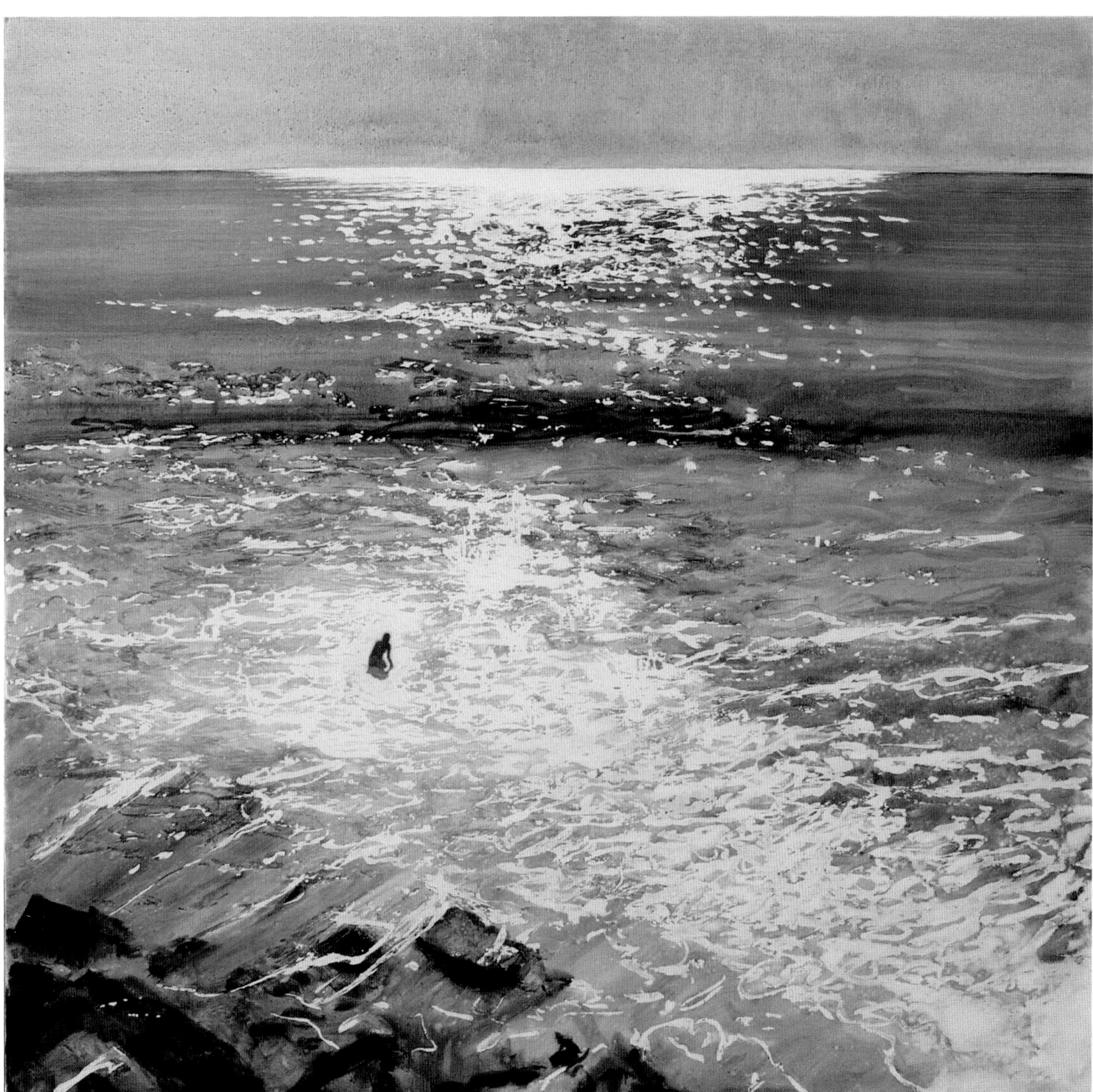

Marguerite Horner (b. 1954) is a British artist based in London who graduated with an MA in Fine Art from City & Guilds of London Art School in 2004. In 2011, she exhibited at the 54th Venice Biennale with WW Gallery and in 2019 at the 58th with Caroline Wiseman Modern and Contemporary. Horner won the MS Amlin Continuity Prize in 2017, part of the National Open Art (NOA) competition, and the British Women Artists Award in 2018. She has exhibited across China, Ireland, Poland, Romania, the UK and the USA, and her work has been acquired by several museums, including the Yale Center for British Art, New Haven, USA.

Dr Matthew Holman holds a PhD in American art history from University College London, and is currently Lecturer in Literature and Fine Arts at the University of Hertfordshire. Matthew regularly writes criticism for the *Art Newspaper*, *frieze*, the *Times Literary Supplement* and elsewhere. His book, *Frank O'Hara: Curator of Modern Life*, is forthcoming with Bloomsbury. https://matthewjamesholman.com/

Matt Price is a London-based publisher, editor and writer. He holds a BA in art history from the University of Nottingham and an MA in curating from the Royal College of Art, London. His writing has featured in magazines such as *Art Monthly*, *ArtReview*, *frieze* and *Flash Art*, and he is a regular contributor to *Art Quarterly*, the magazine of Art Fund.

Marguerite Horner
Numinous

Published by Hurtwood Press Limited, London
Part of the Hurtwood Contemporary Artist Series
Commissioning editor: Matt Price
Series editor: Eliza Scott

The Hurtwood Contemporary Artist Series aims to spotlight a talented and diverse range of artists whether established or early in their careers. Each publication showcases a significant body of work or exhibition by a single artist with high-quality reproductions, and features a foreword and an essay by leading writers and curators. Dynamic and forward looking, Hurtwood's Contemporary Artist Series responds to culture as it happens, documenting the work of artists working nationally and internationally today.

Artist acknowledgements: *Numinous* is dedicated to my four children, Holly, Harvey, Harriet and Hope. I would like to thank everyone at Hurtwood involved in the making of the book, including Roger Jones, Eliza Scott and Agatha Smith. Special thanks are due to Francis Atterbury whose inspired idea it was to make *Numinous*, and to Matthew Holman and Matt Price for their brilliant writing. Thank you to art collectors Debra and Larry Poteet for inviting me to stay in Del Mar and introducing me to the Californian coastline, to the Revd Canon Dr Stephen Evans, Rector of St Marylebone, for giving me an exhibition space for *Numinous*, and to Alex Westlake for building me a studio in my garden, in which I made these works. Thank you lastly to Rudolf Otto for defining the idea of the 'numinous'.

Project editor: Eliza Scott
Proofreading: Matt Price
Design: Agatha Smith
Reprography and production: Hurtwood Press

Published in 2023 by Hurtwood Press Limited, London
© Hurtwood Press Limited, London

ISBN 978-0-903696-77-7

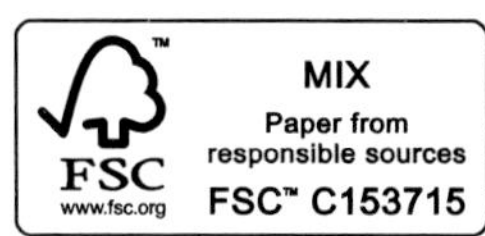

Printed and bound in the UK by Kingsbury Press, using FSC™ Mix

Cover image:
Honour by Silence, 2023 (detail)
Watercolour on paper, 20 x 20 cm (7 ⅞ x 7 ⅞ in.)